ACAPPELLA

LIVING IN THE SHADOWS

1963-1973

A SOCIAL HISTORY

ABRAHAM J. SANTIAGO

HARBINGER PRESS

HARBINGER PRESS

ACAPPELLA LIVING IN THE SHADOWS 1963-1973 A Social History by Abraham J. Santiago

Harbinger Press 400 Greenbay Rd #105 Glencoe, IL 60022 USA

Latin American address: P.O. Box 126 Guaynabo, Puerto Rico 00970-0126 Email: msproductions66@yahoo.com

Printed and bound in the United States of America

Library of Congress Control Number: 2016907271

Create Space Independent Publishing Platform

Front cover artwork: Misa Patricia

Back cover artwork: Horace Pippin (Courtesy of Oberlin College – Allen Memorial Art Museum)

Santiago, Abraham J.

ISBN-13: 978-1516910854 (trade paper)

Title ID: 5679235

Library of Congress Cataloging-in-Publication Data

First Edition

Contains bibliography and index

Doo-Wop-Music- United States-History and Criticism

ACKNOWLEDGEMENTS

I would like to express my deep appreciation to all historians, authors, vocal group singers, journalist, universities, colleges, radio personalities, recording engineers, web sites, clubs, record shops, and organizations that have promoted the R&B group sound and specifically acappella. I deeply appreciate everyone's devotion and commitment to advancing group harmony singing. I want to thank past and present individuals who were there for me in this endeavor. I realize that I may have missed some people and I do apologize. I want to thank Jersey City Public Library, Oberlin College, Northwestern University, Wayne Stierle, New York Public Library, Stan Krause, Jon Rich, Deke Sharon, Contemporary A cappella Society, Glencoe Public Library, Bob Davis, Maurice Kitchen, Julie Hurwitz, Jerry Lawson, Tommy Mitchel, Joe Calamito, Frederick J. Amoroso Jr., Kenneth Bank, Edwin Rivera, Juan Perez, George Scott, John Beekman, Mike Miller, Val Shively, Richard and Marie Orisak, Patricia Meidel, Steve Willette, Indiana University, Marv Goldberg, Steve Yohe, Eddie Black, LHOC men's group, Artistic Digital, University of Puerto Rico, Evanston Public Library. Doo-Wop/Oldies Forum, John Bertelsmeier.

DEDICATED TO SANDY

MOTHER AND GRANDMOTHER OF MY CHILDREN

Charm is deceitful, and beauty is vain,

But a woman who fears the Lord, she shall be praised.

Proverbs 31:30

NIV

&

IN MEMORY OF

STAN R. KRAUSE

ACAPPELLA PIONEER

Table of Contents

INTRODUCTION 1

PART ONE... THE GOLDEN AGE OF ACAPPELLA

CHAPTER 1: THE ROOTS OF ACAPPELLA 12

CHAPTER 2: WE ARE FAMILY 51

CHAPTER 3: DEBUNKING THE PROFESSIONAL MYTH.............. 73

CHAPTER 4: GERIATRIC SINGERS 102

PART TWO... BROTHERS OF ANOTHER SHADE

CHAPTER 5: HISPANIC CONTRIBUTION TO RHYTHM AND BLUES 119

CHAPTER 6: ITALIAN CONNECTION TO RHYTHM AND BLUES 129

CHAPTER 7: JEWISH IMPACT ON RHYTHM AND BLUES 137

PART THREE... MUSICAL JOURNEY

CHAPTER 8: MIKE MILLER 156

CHAPTER 9: JERRY LAWSON 179

CHAPTER 10: JOE CALAMITO 183

CHAPTER 11: EDWIN F. RIVERA 187

CHAPTER 12: VAL SHIVELY 194

CHAPTER 13: KENNETH BANK 198

PART FOUR... PAST, PRESENT, AND FUTURE

CHAPTER 14: NEWARK AND BOWERS AVENUE......................... 205

CHAPTER 15: THE HEALING POWER OF GOOD MUSIC 214

PART FIVE… FINDING MY ECHO

CHAPTER 16: ALBUMS, PHOTOS, PEOPLE, AND EVENTS 223

CHAPTER 17: TEENS, YOUNG ADULTS, AND SOULFUL ARTISTS 244

CHAPTER 18: CHART AND TIMELINE 267

CHAPTER 19: CONTEMPORARY VOCAL GROUPS.................................. 269

CHAPTER 20: JERSEY CITY ON THE HUDSON 282

CHAPTER 21: DISCOGRAPHY... 291

CHAPTER 22: ETHNOGRAPHIC DISCOGRAPHY 363

WORK CITED... 367

ABOUT THE AUTHOR... 372

APPENDIX... 373

INDEX... 376

INTRODUCTION

Vocal group harmonization has come a long way in the vocabulary of American music enthusiasts. This book is about vocal group singing as a pop genre. My goal in writing this tome is to introduce acappella as part of our musical heritage. This book is the first work about acappella within the context of social history, as it pertains to rhythm and blues. When one thinks of acappella, there are two narratives that people most often make a connection to.

First, there is the traditional ecclesiastical choral ensemble, or choir, of the Renaissance period 1450-1600, a time that many considered to be an age of individualism, adventure, curiosity, and human creativity. The second understanding is a more general view where universities, colleges, and contemporary performers sing all sorts of styles without musical instrumentation. This book is about the third tier of style that gave birth to acappella as a new pop art form, and began over fifty years ago. It has no connection with the Renaissance period regarding vocal style; however, it does share some of the same traits like adventure, curiosity, and individualism.

The history of contemporary acappella as a pop genre is not old; it was molded and shaped by the cultural revolution of the 1960s. The roots of acappella goes back to the neighborhoods of prominent cities and hamlets where African-American young adults would gather after church, work, or school and sing. This book, as you will discover, showcases what acappella produced as a pop style that began during that period. Acappella during the 1960s was living in the shadows of other larger-than-life popular genres. It was doing its own thing. My initial goal was to write about non-African-Americans' contribution to rhythm and blues as a separate book. However, what I decided to do was to include what I wrote about non-African Americans in this book as well. Over fifty years have passed since acappella was first introduced to the public on the airwaves, on TV, in theaters, and in record shops.

Today it has become a staple diet for most people, both young and old. I have included, in general, all aspects of music as it pertains to acappella in some fashion. This book will include small elements of jazz, blues, soul and everything in between. I have attempted to cover and connect different musical genres and people. It is a daunting task, trying to look at various musical styles and connect them with group singing in some fashion, for R&B in particular.

As you read this book, I have also included small vignettes of music to clarify, add, or give some insight into the vocal group culture and music as a whole. I have included those who played a part in it within a general social context. The word acappella before its usage in the 1960s in inner-cities was unknown to urban young people. When teens or young adults came together to sing, it was whatever word they came up with. Some called it harmonizing; others called it chords, tunes, notes, or whatever word they used to reflect singing in three or four-part harmony. I say this because, some may have the impression that it was a common term used by urban young people. Young people did not use that word when they came together to sing. Acappella today has evolved and redefined itself; it does not have the same meaning as when it first appeared in the 1960s. Today, what was once called acappella when groups came together to sing in the R&B style, we nowadays call it Doo-Wop.

Hopefully, this book will help us better understand the development of contemporary acappella as a popular genre from its beginning during the turbulent years of the '60s. The acappella era of the 1960s set the stage for the vocal group rivals of the late 1970s, 1980s and beyond. For the record, acappella was not a cultural or counter-movement during the 1960s; rather it was a spontaneous, unrehearsed group of young artists singing in the public domain.

Lastly, I have included some articles in this work that was published in the past. Furthermore, the spelling of acappella that I am using in this book is what Irving Slim Rose devised when he launched this undertaking. With that said, let us take a trip back into the past, and trace acappella as a new pop genre of the 1960s and discover the music it made. Join me now as we take a musical journey back in time, and rediscover vocal group harmony.

In perfect harmony,

Abraham J. Santiago

"If acappella hadn't become popular in the 1960s, many talented performers might never have had a chance to contribute to vocal group history."

-Jay Warner

"You see acapella represents black music in all of its raw and naked glory."

-Bob Davis

"With the a cappella groups, every voice is like one string on a guitar, one note on the piano, or one cymbal, and you don't have the luxury of falling back on anything."

-Ben Folds

PART ONE

THE GOLDEN AGE

OF ACAPPELLA

1

THE ROOTS OF ACAPPELLA

"Let's hit some notes and see if we can draw a crowd."

In order to understand the origin of acappella as an urban pop musical art form, we need to go back into the past and travel to the segregated southern states like Mississippi, Georgia, the Carolinas, and Alabama. It is in these and other Southern states that we can begin to understand the historical background of acappella's development. In the twentieth century, the north experienced an influx of black migration from the Southern states. Black folks were looking for employment and a chance to advance themselves socially and economically. A massive migration of African Americans went north after the First World War in 1918. Between 1918 and 1930, many African Americans moved to eastern cities. A second movement followed this first migration between 1940 and 1970. It is in this context, of coming to the northeastern states that we can see a glimpse of black cultural music coming to urban America. African American cultural roots in the church and slavery, as well as musical rhythmic roots from Africa, contributed to what we today call "acappella" as an urban folk-pop genre.

Perhaps the best well-known example of African Americans coming north and engaging in singing acappella style is in the artwork done by African American artist Horace Pippin from West Chester, Pennsylvania. In his painting, Pippin portrays four young men standing on the corner of West Gay and Hannum streets in West Chester. This art perhaps embodies the very heart of vocal group harmony: young men coming together to sing. His painting is rightly called *Harmonizing* and this is what singing on street corners was called during his time. Other terms were used, but it never was called "acappella" or the onomatopoeic term "doo-wop," which we use today for this style of singing. Techniques like nonsense syllables and creating chords to fill in space were utilized in this style of singing. Vocal instrumentation, beat-boxing, or vocal percussion was never used; it did not exist when acappella became popular in urban cities on the East Coast in the 1960s.

When African Americans began to move to the eastern cities, a cultural exchange took place and a new distinctiveness formed. Many families were discriminated against when entering white neighborhoods. It was not like the South, yet they could feel that whites did not want "their kind" in the community. There are many reasons why this racial attitude prevailed, but fear was probably the dominant reason whites were reluctant to associate with their new black neighbors. Fear of losing jobs to newcomers, social contact, and dating was probably on the list for many people. It was a repeat of what Catholics experienced during the turn of the nineteenth century, when they were discriminated against for being Roman Catholic and emigrants from Europe with different cultural traits. Yet, the very people who discriminated against black families were the descendants of those who were discriminated against for being foreigners and Catholics; a depressing commentary on race relations. Nevertheless, within the borders of their own neighborhoods, blacks grew and developed their own resourceful spirit. They built churches, schools, and universities, started businesses, created their own social clubs, and assimilated themselves within the white establishment as best they could.

Horace Pippin (1888 – 1946 West Chester, Pennsylvania),
Harmonizing

(Courtesy of Oberlin College – Allen Memorial Art Museum)

We don't have to go back many years to see this. If we start during the first wave of black migration from 1918–1930, we can get a glimpse and a sense of the yearning felt among African-Americans who left the South to advance themselves and escape the Jim Crow laws and the discrimination that existed in their southern communities. Perhaps the best place to begin the search for black advancement and the birth of urban folk music is New York City, specifically Harlem. Harlem was the place where the black experience fermented and, to a certain degree, street corner singing or vocal group harmonization, sprouted its seed of singing. Keep in mind that African Americans, wherever they went, managed to impregnate their surrounding community with their cultural mores and music. Along the Eastern Seaboard corridor, the colored man became a symbol of the new man. This can be attested to by the fact that many white ethnic communities supposedly feared rock 'n' roll and the new moniker rhythm and blues as colored music. They wanted no part of colored music influencing their teenagers. Harlem became the epicenter for the New Negro, along with Philadelphia, Chicago, Detroit, and a few other cities. It was in Harlem that musicians, writers, actors, singers, intellectuals, and poets dominated the sphere of the black populace. It was the Harlem Renaissance in the making. It is within this historical context that aspiring singers and musicians sought to sing or play in places like the Cotton Club, the Savoy Ballroom, Stork Club and the Apollo Theater. The non-African American fascination with the exotic world of blackness in Harlem during this period created a sense of curiosity and admiration. Within this setting, aspiring young people burst forth into the limelight with hopes of being like Langston Hughes, Wallace Thurman, Nella Larsen, Zora Neale Hurston, and many others.

Singing was part of the strategy for some young people who could not enter clubs because they were underage. They used their talent to get into clubs and bypass the legal entry age. The legal age of entry into clubs and buying liquor was eighteen. It was New York City and the surrounding urban communities that made it possible for young people to explore the field of entertainment. Although there were many forms of entertainment, like the famous Lindy Hoppers dance crew, if the average black young adult in urban America could sing or play an instrument, that was all he needed. It was on the Eastern Coast of urban America more than any other region that vocal group singing set its roots and developed. That is why vocal group harmonization has always been considered an East

Coast genre. Yet, colored music had no place for the WASP establishment.[1] If anything, it was considered to be degenerate music. Jazz, blues, dance, art, and anything connected to colored people was considered low art. The German phrase for degenerate art, *entartete kunst* is what some called this type of art. This was a term used by the Nazis later on. This is what some upper crust of American society believed, and to a certain degree, so did some blue-collar middle-class Americans, like the 1970s TV character Archie Bunker. Black music and socialization in any form was threatening to their staunch European ethnocentric views. An invisible wall existed bound by race, social mores and, in some cases, religion. This social climate led some young people to be inspired, to become an aspiring singer in some fashion, as either a soloist, a member of a vocal group or band. With this perspective, we can trace some of the steps that led to, or laid the foundation for, singing on street corners among urban young people. They became, to a small degree, a catalyst for change, with impromptu unrehearsed singing in public squares.

http://www.heartlandbrewery.com/

---

[1] Note: A term which means White Anglo Saxon Protestant; usually refers to people in power or high status.

THE REASON

New York Public Library

(Courtesy Schomberg Center for Research in Black Culture)

The question some may ask is this, how did "low art music" become an accepted art form among white middle- and upper-class society? What were the changes that led society to accept this new "colored" music? Perhaps it was the music coming out of Harlem in the form of the big band sound, jazz, dance, and soloist singing that contributed to the acceptance of this new art form. The music during the Harlem Renaissance did attract white progressives and intellectuals to side with colored folks. It was more the upper crust, which, for the most part, accepted this new art form. Liberal-thinking individuals who viewed black people as having an inner creative spirit and the ability to convey that in the form of art, literature and music were the first to write about Negros in general. They became the vanguard in changing the negative sentiment among whites into something positive. It should be noted that radio also played a part in introducing black music to the public. However, more than that, some believed that a profit could be made by utilizing and exploiting black people and their raw talent. A brief analysis of the business that employed Negro talent reveals that the music industry was primarily owned and operated by Europeans. In the end, African Americans were used to enrich the pockets of white business owners who saw African Americans as being creative but lacking the business expertise to sustain them for the long haul.

It is also not surprising to find that many of the record shops, clubs, radio stations, and theaters in Harlem were owned by whites. It is no surprise either that many record companies were owned and operated by non-African Americans who saw an opportunity to make a profit and capitalize on the black man's talent. This was the opening that non-African Americans saw and exploited. New raw talent opened the doors for white businessmen to take advantage of it. For non-blacks, money was the key ingredient into becoming affluent at the expense of others. They deemed this, to some extent, as being part of the American Dream: find an opportunity, create a niche, and develop what you have. And so, African Americans jumped into the arena of music and mimicked their Caucasian counterparts. The end result was the building of black-owned businesses like insurance companies, funeral parlors, restaurants, and newspapers.[2] Unfortunately, many African Americans who were employed by black businessmen were not treated fairly and indeed, in some cases, white folks treated black talent much better. African-Americans learned the necessary skills in running a business from their counterparts. Some preferred managing black talent and becoming the middlemen for white business owners, others started their own labels. It is within these boundaries that vocal group singing on street corners caught the eye of potential negotiators, who we now call A&R, who enlisted potential singers into the sleazy world of music.[3]

The Queens

---

[2]http://www.theroot.com/articles/history/2014/03/black_newspapers_which_one_was_the_first. html

[3] Note: Artists and repertoire (A&R) is responsible for talent scouting and overseeing the artistic development of songwriters or recording artists within the record industry.

Lindy Hoppers

Billie Holiday, 1937 – Apollo Theater with Count Basie

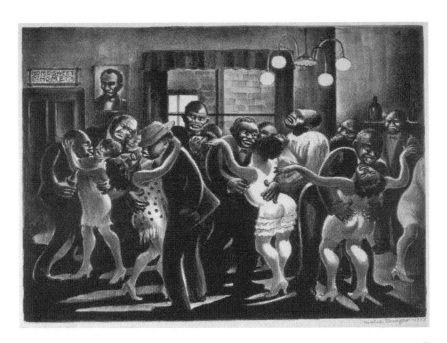

Mabel Dwight, 1929 – Harlem Rent Party

Joe DiMaggio at the Cotton Club 1937

http://www.heartlandbrewery.com/

It is within this social-cultural context that would-be black entertainers and future artists would pay their dues in some fashion to become potential stars. Many had to work long hours as cocktail servers, domestic workers, or give up their bodies to wealthy white men to enjoy. Others worked as dishwashers, bouncers, bookies, and janitors, knowing that there might be a chance to make it in the entertainment world of Harlem. This was not the only place where talent could be found. By the late 1940s and into the 1950s, high schools became a melting pot of young moldable raw talent. Middlemen in the shady world of music were out looking for potential entertainers who would be interested in playing in clubs, theaters, or dives where customers could come and be entertained by black folks. It was a talent agent's dream to secure gifted and talented minors and introduce them to the mendacious world of music. Keep in mind that young adults were still under the influence of their parents and family. Black teenagers and adolescents in general were viewed as a high priority for potential advancement in music. There were many high schools throughout the acappella corridor that had budding talent. One high school in particular in Jersey City was known for producing great and exceptional musical talent, James J. Ferris high school was one of them. Ferris produced groups like The Emeralds, Valentines, Concepts, Medallions, Heartaches, and many others. However, the same mindset of the past decade continued during the turbulent years of the 1960s and beyond.

Dancing the night away (circa 1950s)

ACAPPELLA REDEFINED

Contemporary acappella as a pop genre came out of the cultural rock 'n' roll ethos of the 1950s. As a distinct pop genre, acappella began during the civil and social unrest of the 1960s.[4] Street-corner groups inherited, to some degree, the values of that time period. Vocal groups during the 1960s sought out their own ethnic-racial types to join their groups and also any potential person who could sing, regardless of color or ethnicity. The moniker "white people" was still not a distinguishable term among ethnic groups along the acappella corridor. Ethnic groups still referred to others by their ethnic heritage: Italian, Polish, Jewish, Irish, etc. African Americans

---

[4] http://www.casa.org/node/6160 The CASA – Contemporary A cappella Society – maintains that a cappella is not a genre but a musical performance style.

were still called colored, never black or African American until the late 1960s and into the 1980s.[5] All of these factors were woven into the social fabric of the time. In addition, the political and social upheaval contributed to songs sung by acappella groups. A case in point is the song recorded by the lead singer of the Persuasions, Jerry Lawson. The song "Hymn #9" was a big hit in Oakland, California, home of the radical group the Black Panthers. The song was written by James Shaw and his wife Delia Gartrell. The Black Panthers and others saw the song as an acappella groove, a testimony to the Vietnam conflict and black struggle. This song became the very first acappella recording about the Vietnam war that spoke about the aftermath of black soldiers coming home.

[5] http://www.nytimes.com/1989/01/31/us/african-american-favored-by-many-of-america-s-blacks.html?pagewante d=all

The Persuasions

When soul music came on the scene as a new pop genre, acapella shared the same roots as soul music and the two have a symbiotic relationship. The vocal group Royal Counts produced two eclectic albums entitled Acappella Soul volumes 1 and 2, consisting of popular songs from the 1950s and contemporary songs of the 1960s. Jersey City and New York City were the breeding grounds that gave birth to the modern art form we today commonly call contemporary acappella. Acappella during the 1960s exploded and replicated itself like an infection spreading from Boston to Pittsburgh on what is now called the acappella corridor. The epicenter for acappella was not churches or colleges, but subway platforms, hallways, bathrooms, and street corners. It was in these unassuming spots that young adults sang in the R&B harmony style of the 1950s, copying the African American groups and adding their own curvature to the songs. Today that style of music is called doo-wop. For the record, many vocal groups had an eclectic repertoire, their songs consisted of Broadway hits to soul and everything in-between. Vocal group singing in the R&B 1950s style had no signature name. However, some vocal group aficionados maintain that the term doo-wop was used during the late 1950s and into the early 1960s to describe black rhythm and blues singing. Gribin and Schiff write:

"When I first started to hear the term Doo-Wop used in the late fifties and early sixties, it was primarily used to describe the white group sound of that time. But slowly over the years, the black group sound of the late forties and early fifties has been placed under the Doo-Wop label instead of rhythm and blues. Thus, the term rhythm and blues was supplanted over the years, perhaps for the sake of simplicity, with doo–wop." [6]

The vast majority of vocal group enthusiasts and historians would argue with Gribin and Schiff as to when the term doo-wop was first used to define rhythm and blues vocal group singing. There appears to be insufficient evidence, if any, to prove the use of the term to describe R&B vocal group singing. It was in 1970, not before, that the term doo-wop became a new moniker to describe vocal group singing in the rhythm and blues style. Radio DJs did not refer to R&B group singing as doo-wop. It is not a 1950s or 60s term; Gus Gossert, a DJ from New York City, was encouraged by Stan Krause and Wayne

---

[6] Anthony J. Gribin and Matthew M. Schiff – The Complete Book of Doo-Wop 2000 Krause Publications pg.9

Stierle to use the word, and he introduced it on the radio. It should be noted, that Stierle and Krause were the music advisors and archival directors for the show. Krause saw the word on an LP that featured a compilation of vocal groups from Los Angeles. Krause and Stierle believed that if the term doo-wop was used, it would attract and bring radio listeners to his show since there was no official signature name for that genre. For the sake of clarity, Stierle was the first to use doo-wop on an album series in 1970. Keep in mind that the moniker to describe rhythm and blues vocal group harmonization from the 1940s to 1970 had no official classification. No name existed; however, from 1963 to 1970 there was already a loosely established description: it was acappella and became perhaps the most prominent name category used in print and on the radio to describe singing in the R&B style. A case could be made that acappella was the loose generic term used to describe rhythm and blues group singing, with or without band instrumentation. Other terms were used, but doo-wop was not one of them. With this said, acappella meant group singing in the rhythm and blues style. It became the unofficial colloquial name as the genre started to grow along the acappella corridor. Acappella was understood as group singing in the rhythm and blues mold. We can say unequivocally that before hip hop, rap, and doo-wop, there was acappella.

It is important to understand that singing on street corners or playing music in public during the 1960s and early 1970s, especially in New York City, was an outlet for performers who attracted many people. Street artists, mostly young adults, did dances and pantomime, musicians played guitars, brass, or percussion. Many of these street artists were panhandlers who performed for money or small change. Vocal groups used public spaces as their open-air theater too. However, they never panhandled because they sang strictly for pleasure and to pick up lovely young women. Gribin and Schiff write:

"Singing on street corners was meant to impress; it was a social thing that helped established the group's turf, to pull ranks in friends, not in the group, and to show off to the ladies".[7]

It is in this context that the narrative of acappella emerged. The year was 1963, and it was Irving "Slim" Rose of Times Square Records in New York City who coined the term acappella to define 1950s rhythm and blues vocal group singing without music. Wayne Stierle, an employee at Times Square Records on 42nd Street, was arranging a record deal. In his deal, a collection of master reel-to-reel tapes was included; this was something he set up with his friend Don Fileti. Stierle could not afford to buy the tapes, so Slim bought them. In this batch of master tapes were vocal recordings with no band or orchestra, which no one knew. Tapes without a band were frequently used by record companies as demos to hear how a group sounded.

---

[7] Ibid. Pg.185

28

If the group seemed first-class, musicians would add music to these demo tapes, or practice tapes as they were often called in the 1950s. Slim played some of these recordings in his record shop and there was a great interest in the music. These practice tapes had no name as a genre, so Stierle came up with a designation to describe R&B group singing in the 1950s style without music.

Stierle suggested "subway sound" or "street corner sound", or something like it, which would explain the vocals with no music. Slim did not want people returning records and saying they had no music, so he looked in the dictionary and found the word "a cappella." Slim changed the spelling to acappella[8] and took the recordings and released them on his Times Square label as acappella. The new art form began to grow and found its way onto the airwaves on station WBNX 1380 and others. Before long, radio stations like WHOM and WCAM were playing acappella recordings made by various groups trying to get a bigger audience. The unexpected increase in popularity of this new musical style exploded. A new art form of singing was introduced to the already crowded multitude of classification styles. Acappella joined the ranks of other categories competing for a fan base and exposing a new style of singing to the public at large. Acapella artists were living in the shadows of the big music makers and competing with them.

---

[8] Author's note: A cappella was spelled with a space after the first letter A. "Slim" joined the whole word together with no space, creating, in a sense, a new word.

Stan Krause and Ron Luciano at the Fox Theater

Authenticity

One of the chief complaints by some vocal group enthusiasts is that many of the acappella artists who sang well lacked the "black indigenous sound." They sounded "white," as if "white" was inferior to black or that "whiteness" has a sound of its own. Joel Rudinow comments:

"And so the criteria for authenticity have been understood in terms of accuracy or conformity with performance specifications that constitute a work".[9]

Clearly, race should not be an issue; however, for some purists, it matters. The vocal group purists preferred the vocal sound coming from black groups to white ethnic groups. Ethnic groups who sang songs traditionally sung by black groups were considered imitations, not the real thing. In a short time, as the momentum continued, more non-African American groups joined the ranks of this new sound.

As a genre, acappella, for the most part, became an R&B genus singing style composed mostly of ethnic groups and a sprinkling of black groups. The result is that an industry emerged with all the trappings of success and a future. This new and emerging industry was clearly independent. The record labels produced acappella artists, creating a *"groove"* in the music industry dominated by Detroit, Memphis, and other regional sounds. This groove was not seen as an opportunity to

---

[9] Joel Rudinow – Soul Music: Tracking the Spiritual Roots of Pop from Plato to Motown University of Michigan Press pg.133.

Note: Keep in mind that there were acappella recordings that were made on the Decca label during WWII. The vocal group Song Spinners made it into the pop charts in 1943 to promote the war effort.

advance a new urban pop genre and vocal music by established record companies. Record companies instead saw it as a fad and totally snubbed those who were trying to promote this genre. Keep in mind that many acappella artists of the 1960s did not have the "black-soulful sound" as entertainers. Ethnic groups of that generation did not have rising soulful singers like Robin Thicke or Elliot Yamin as we have today. Those vocal artists sang with what they had, and never attempted to imitate a "soul sound" which they knew they did not have. They sang it as best as they could and made sure the arrangements and harmonies were tight. The only exception was U.N. groups, with their racial and ethnic mix.

Fortunately, the genre did catch on and became an established commercial success along the acappella corridor. In actuality, it became a million-dollar business divided between all the record companies that emerged within a ten-year-plus period, and was small but profitable. Part of their success was how acappella marketed itself. Acappella record companies did not have what one would call today a marketing strategy. The record company owners were all young, under twenty-five. Their goal in marketing is what one would call the store price marketing strategy.

Long-Playing Acappella Versus Industry Long-Playing Records

Packaging popular music during the 1960s and making it appealing to the public was a major goal among record companies. Throughout the 1950s, the 45-rpm single was supreme and it always had the potential to become a major hit. However, by the mid-sixties, the 45-rpm started to wane and the long-playing album (LP) began to take a more prominent position. What made the acappella era unique during the height of the sixties was the new concept of promoting and packaging long-playing albums. Mainstream record companies had quite an advantage when it came to marketing. They knew how to market and they had the best artists, photographers and graphic designers for their albums. Many of the album covers during the 1960s crossed the spectrum from traditional to risqué. In addition, many albums had a social or cultural element displayed on their covers. Acappella record companies could not compete with the majors on this level. They had no Madison Avenue sales people or designers. However, they were street smart, and showed their brilliance by attacking and ambushing the mainstream companies from the rear with their street-smart agility.

The standard record industry concept of packaging (LPs) was to produce twelve songs on an album with one artist or group on black vinyl. The acappella record companies differed radically from mainstream record companies in packaging and promoting their performers. Their street smarts mindset, allowed them to out-think their competitors. They developed a different and innovative approach in packaging and advancing their artists. Here is where the theory of deferential advantage in marketing comes in, and takes over. Their technique was to produce twenty songs instead of the standard twelve songs mainstream record companies were offering. They also included more artists, usually five or more on albums, instead of the standard one artist or group. Moreover, acappella record companies issued vinyl albums and 45s of various colors along with the standard black vinyl.

It worked. Why pay for twelve songs and hear one group, when you can hear twenty songs by five or more groups for the same price of a single album? This concept blew major record companies out of the ballpark. They could not compete with this store price marketing strategy. Eventually the majors on a small scale did it with two groups or more competing with each other on the same album, like the Paragons and the Jesters, or the Cadillac's and the Orioles, but not with an array of songs like those that the acappella industry produced. The major record companies missed out on capitalizing on this very innovative idea brought by the new and daring independent acappella record companies. All this contributed to the excitement and preservation of the group sound. It was these assets which made the acappella era unique in music during the 1960s. All this was developed, for the most part, by young men who had no university or college education. In the end, the record conglomerates lost out. The established major record labels missed the opportunity to take advantage of the first folk urban acappella pop genre. What happened as a result of this was the emergence of a new sound: The Hudson Sound. The emerging new musical sound was competing with the big sounds of Detroit, British, Folk, Memphis, and other regional sounds. The major labels could have taken the 1950s groups that they discarded and made them successful and recorded them as acappella. Record companies chose not to reinvest in their artists, and the only 1950s group that made an LP acappella recording was The Shells. They were the first professional group from the 1950s to produce an acappella album on the Candlelite label, created by Wayne Stierle. It was perhaps one of the biggest failures of the major record companies, not reinventing in the vocal group artists they had.

Nick and the Nacks

Nicholas Sudano

Irving "Slim" Rose at United Group Harmony Association
1979

It is within this social context, that contemporary acappella as a new pop genre, became an industry within the current historical background of the 1960s. Irving "Slim" Rose did not know at that time that his companions and employees were embarking on a new journey that would bring acappella into mainstream music, competing with major musical genres of the time. Within this background, acappella group singing surfaced. This undertaking became the starting gate for the successful commercial market that would later give rise to the reissuing of records from the 1950s. It was the impetus for oldies radio programming, and the promotion and preservation of classic rhythm and blues vocal group singing. Prior to this period, there was no record industry that specifically produced acappella recordings for commercial consumption. For the sake of clarity, Decca Records did produce acappella recordings in the 1940s during World War II. The singing group Sound Spinners produced "You'll Never Know" featuring Dick Haymes, which was a big hit, and "Comin' in on a Wing and a Prayer" and "Johnny Zero". The musicians of New York City were on strike and because of this, Decca Records produced some acappella recordings, and it became a national hit. The songwriters Adamson and McHugh wrote several patriotic songs, and it rallied the American people to the war cause.[10]

[10] Leslie M. Alexander and Walter C. Rucker Jr. Encyclopedia of African American History ABC CLO Press 2010 pg.143

Lastly, acappella today has spread from a regional neighborhood sound born on the banks of the Hudson River to five continents. For over fifty years, industry moguls have considered acappella to be an undertaking not worth investing in. However, that has changed, and people realize that there is potential commercial profit to be made by promoting acappella.

Acappella and Vocal Group Resurgence

With this in mind, we cannot forget the decade of the 1970s and beyond when there was a resurgence of vocal group revival taking place. It was during this time period that acappella singing groups came back with a vocal vengeance. It was the war in Vietnam that gave many groups a hiatus, and now those groups of the past as well as new groups were back. It was during this time period that the various vocal groups brought contemporary acappella back to the public domain. There were three factors that led to the vocal group resurgence. One was the acappella era in general, the second was Ralph Nader's "Rock and Roll Rival" and then there was radio disc-jockey Gus Gossert of WCBS AND WPIX, radio who launched the vocal group sound to a new audience. During the decade of the 1970s and beyond, hundreds of vocal groups were performing up and down the acappella corridor. Acappella record labels were sprouting on fertile ground and people were hungry to hear vocal group harmonization and especially acappella. Record labels like U.G.H.A. Starlight, Avenue D, Blue Sky, Relic, and many others were turning out recordings. Show promoters like the late Ralph Nader were filling arenas like Madison Square Garden with classic old school entertainment, along with acappella groups. It was a big business and contemporary acappella was being highlighted. A multitude of acappella singing groups were being showcased and their fans came to see them perform. Sadly, the mainstream music industry did not find them worthy of being on their label. They were still operating under the assumption that acappella was not a profitable or marketable enterprise. This mind set continued to hamper singing groups and the end result was that artists continued to record for independent acappella record labels.

Ambassadors to Acappella

The leader of the pack within this time frame were the Persuasions. Keep in mind that other acappella groups were right up there with the Persuasions, but they had the upper hand because their songs of choice were eclectic in nature. They did not adhere to a specific rhythm and blues genre which we call doo–wop.

They sang anything and everything and made it their own with their soulful gritty style. The Persuasions in the 1970s and beyond set the standard for contemporary acappella and the pop genre we have today. They were the only official pop/soul contemporary vocal group that was singing hits and songs of current artists of that period. Keep in mind again that there were other acappella groups, but the Persuasions were a genuine group that was not on an independent acappella record label; they recorded for major record companies.

In the decade of the 1970s, the Persuasions were the ambassadors to the relatively new independent acappella record industry that was started in the '60s. The Persuasions were the only acappella group of the 1960s and 1970s who recorded for independent acappella labels, and then for major record companies, first for a major record company Straight and then Capitol records. During the '70s, the Persuasions released nine albums. David Dashev became the Persuasions' first producer and manager for a major record label in the 1970s. It was a marriage made in heaven. Dashev took the Persuasions on tour across the country and into colleges and universities and introduced acappella urban style to students. The Persuasions became the catalyst for reintroducing acappella in a fresh and unique way to young people thanks to

Dashev's connections and expertise in managing and arranging. It was Dashev's enthusiasm, and friendship that propelled the Persuasions to heights of popularity. It was his molding of the Persuasions in their early embryonic career that made them who they are today. They were the only contemporary acappella group that was receiving that much attention. The Persuasions in the '70s made the top 100 albums in Rolling Stone magazine, a feat that no acappella group ever made. This clearly tells us that the Persuasions set the tone for what we have today within the acappella genre.

Moreover, the Persuasions were partially influential in promoting the new urban folk sound Hudson; a new urban inner city sound, that was competing with other regional sounds like Motown, Country, British, Memphis, Psychedelic rock, and many others. The Persuasions were singing what disc jockeys were playing on the radio. College acappella ensembles and barbershop groups did not do this; they did not have a voice on commercial radio, nor were they filling theaters and stadiums with young people. The Persuasions reintroduced acappella to colleges in the '70s in a fresh and unique way igniting acappella across the United States. Also, for the sake of clarity, the Persuasions appeared on major TV networks with luminous personalities like the Tonight Show with Johnny Carson. The Persuasions likewise were billed with many top entertainers from major record labels including artists from Frank Zappa to the Temptations. As was said previously, the Persuasions are by far the most influential acappella vocal group of their time. For the record, they never claimed to be a doo-wop group.

Many have labeled the Persuasions as a doo-wop group simply because they are African-Americans.[11] They have recorded what we call today doo-wop classics, but when you examine their discography, it is an eclectic choice of various genres. Their recordings of classic doo-wop songs were very few in number. Clearly their choice of materials to sing was very broad. In addition to their popularity, they were also the mentors to many acappella and non-acappella groups; this includes Talk of the Town, Boyz II Men, Take 6, 14 Karat Soul, Rockapella, and many others. They were the catalyst and inspiration for starting CASA -Contemporary Acappella Society of America. Their eclectic repertoire has drawn from everything from Frank Zappa to The Beatles, to Sam Cook; from country to blues, to rock and jazz. They have, in the words of some, *"Persuasionized"* the materials they sing. It is in this historic context that another contender, Deke Sharon, comes into the neighborhood and fills the void with his love and enthusiasm for acappella. Deke Sharon, the founder of the Contemporary A Cappella Society, is also the vocal producer and arranger of Perfect Pitch and The Sing-Off. He and others like him brought acappella center stage. What has made acappella popular and a success today is that Sharon was able to fill in the sound gap, replicate pounding rhythms, and impersonate instruments. Sharon used his writing skills and arrangements to make acappella more appealing to the masses. Also, he was able to surround himself with like-minded individuals and market acappella. This was perhaps, the missing link in making acappella more attractive to the multitudes. Although acappella

---

[11] https://www.youtube.com/watch?v=NSPbeOiEO3Q

has changed and evolved into something entirely different from its original rhythm and blues origin, it is still developing.

Acappella Keeps Growing and Growing

Some might say the turning point in the popularity of acappella was in the mid-1980s when the singing group Rockapella played a role in the PBS kids' game show Where in the World Is Carmen Sandiego? Their appearance sparked a general public interest in acappella. However, that was not the only spark that started a fire growing. Before Rockapella, and throughout the 1980s and beyond, numerous groups appeared on the scene. One new group that emerged from the Hudson River enclave was the vocal group 14 Karat Soul; a group consisting of five young men who were mentored by Stan Krause, acappella pioneer and Skip Jackson, recording artist and music arranger. This group was also similar to the Persuasions and toured all over Europe and was immensely popular in Japan. The only difference between this group and the Persuasions is that they recorded for an acappella label, Catamount records, and not a major record company. Moreover, for the record, many acappella groups performed in Clifton, New Jersey at the well-known and respected organization U.G.H.A. every month. For thirty-two years, the United Group Harmony Association was one of the few organizations in the United States showcasing rhythm and blues vocal groups. The United Group Harmony Association under the leadership of Ronnie Italiano or Ronnie I, supported acappella artists and showcased them and classic groups from the 1940s to '50s. So clearly, acappella was alive and making strides in the music industry well into the new millennium.

With this said, now we come to the present and the role Deke Sharon has played in acappella today. Deke Sharon is the founder of CASA-Contemporary A Cappella Society of America as was mentioned before. CASA is an organization that is growing by leaps and bounds in the music world. Sharon's love for acappella is undisputed. His love and enthusiasm for the genre is clearly seen in what he has accomplished. However, here is where marketing, a bit of ego and youth comes in and takes over. Sharon has been called the father of contemporary acappella, a term that was bestowed by Entertainment Weekly; that statement is found in the back cover of his new book[12].

For the sake of historical veracity, when you search back fifty plus years, contemporary acappella was already a bourgeoning genre being heard on the radio, with theatres being filled by young people, recordings being made and a flourishing acappella record industry. All this took place along the acappella corridor. With all due respect to his followers, Sharon did not create this present genre, as some have suggested. Sharon popularized it and made it more palpable to the general public. Contemporary acappella had its roots even before Sharon was born. There are a lot of people who played a part in bringing acappella to fruition. However, his introduction to vocal percussion and impersonating instruments, set him apart and gained him notoriety. Also, as was mentioned earlier, his arrangement and writing of musical scores was the thing that captured the hearts of young people, mostly students to his cause. In the same way, Sharon surrounded himself with people who shared the same vision who were willing to think outside

[12] Deke Sharon, Ben Spalding and Brody McDonald. A cappella. Alfred Music. (2015)

the proverbial box and use leverage to his advantage, acappella is growing now because someone has filled the empty gap and that gap was Sharon. It is because of this, and his success, that Sharon is getting a multitude of accolades. Does Sharon deserve the accolades? Yes, as long as it is not at the expense of history, and the pioneers who went before him. Is he the father or Godfather of contemporary acappella? Fortunately, that honor and title is still held by Jerry Lawson. However, since Sharon is in the limelight now, he is the Pezzonovante.[13] With that said, acappella is here to stay.

 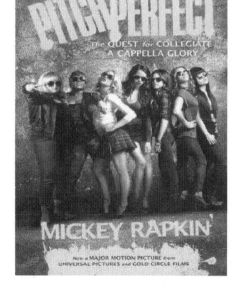

Deke Sharon

---

[13] An Italian word, meaning a man with power. A powerful person or big shot.

Persuasions

(Courtesy of https://chickenlittlecomedy.wordpress.com/photos/)

****

Groove Barbers

****

Jerry Lawson and Gus Gossert

(Courtesy George Scott archives)

Wayne Stierle, Gus Gossert, and Stan Krause

2

WE ARE FAMILY

"Historically, black music has influenced other cultures and other genres."

"Miguel"

The popularity of soul music began in the early 1960s as a fusion of what was going on in the black community. The civil rights movement, black pride, and the attempt to express one's "blackness" help shape soul music. Black music transformed itself from a vocal style by design to a sound form. "Sound" became prominent in soul music rather than vocals. It was the sound coming from the Funk Brothers Band of Motown and the songwriting skills of Holland, Dozier, and Holland that made soul music unique. The Chicago sound, along with Motown, Muscle Shoals and Memphis, helped shape soul music into a new urban pop and regional sound. A great deal of the early music in the 1960s reflected a social commentary on what was happening in America and the world. The Players' song about Vietnam, *"He'll Be Back"*, clearly reflected the period. *"People Get Ready"*, a song on civil rights by The Impressions, was also reflective of the 1960s. *"Say it, Loud, I'm Black and I'm Proud"* on black pride by James Brown mirrored the music that was coming out in the 1960s. We must not forget the urban Blaxploitation films of the early 1970s that featured soundtracks of soul and funk music. They were geared towards an urban black populace and eventually appealed to non-blacks.

The birth of soul can be traced to the partial abandonment of the rhythm and blues four-part 1950s harmony style of singing. This fractional abandoning of vocal group-style harmonization was a rejection of something old for something new by mostly large record labels like Atlantic, Mercury, and Columbia Records. Record companies betrayed many vocal groups from the 1950s. Instead of investing in the groups who made them money, the record companies discarded them. They forsook the groups and began to search for something unique, a new act and sound. They did very little to help groups re-invent themselves. Record companies or so-called "friends" abandoned groups from the 1950s into the cold elements. The birth of soul music with rudiments of gospel and blues was the element producers and record companies were looking for. By way of good connections with disc jockeys, radio stations, a distribution network, and performing on the Chitlin circuit, soul music captured the hearts and ears of America's white middle-class populace. One could say soul music came into existence as a result of the development and innovations of the post-World War II musicians and singers who, fundamentally, turned gospel music into a non-spiritual, secular art form. This new art form was anathema in the minds of many within the African American community. Turning something spiritual that reflected the gospel of Jesus Christ into something secular was something many in the black community considered an affront. Who were these singers and musicians who gambled to upset the established norm? Why would these musicians and singers display disrespect for the religious values of their community? Ray Charles was perhaps one of the first to trample a gospel hymn and make it into a secular song. His first big hit, *"I Got a Woman"*, came from a gospel song originally done by The Southern Tones called *"It Must Be Jesus"*, recorded in 1954 on the Duke label. Ray Charles made this song into a hit by changing the lyrics and keeping the basic melody. It was not hard to do, and it worked. His departure from his upbringing of church music into the secular mode set the tone for others to follow in the same manner. In the end, to some, it was the birth of what we call now soul music. The same could be said of the song "Shout." Ronald Isley says:

"Church groups weren't happy with 'Shout.' We turned a song with a gospel feel into a R&B hit, and the groups began writing to disc jockeys asking them to stop playing our record. They felt 'Shout' should have been a church record".[14]

 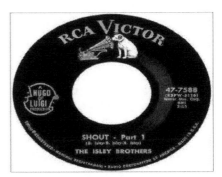

Ray Charles & the Raelettes

Ray Charles provided the skeleton for the new musical genre of soul in the 1950s. What followed Ray Charles were singers who stepped up to the plate and offered the same modification from gospel to secular. James Brown, an admirer of Ray Charles, became the catalyst for the new up-and-coming genre. It was

---

[14] http://www.wsj.com/articles/how-the-isley-brothers-created-shout-1446572577

Brown who eventually became the Godfather of Soul and brought it to another level. His raw vocals, dance steps, a rhythmic band with brass horns and lyrical message made his sound unique. Another pioneer who influenced many is Sister Rosetta Tharpe, who blended religious gospel music with secular music. Tharpe was one of the few early female blues guitarists of her era.[15] However, the real flesh and blood of soul came out of Detroit and provided the breath of life. Soul music became a living sound for all of America. What followed Charles were singers, musicians, and record companies merging into soulful regional sounds. These variations and styles of soul music captured the young people of America and the world. Soul distinguished itself by a few key features. In the beginning, there was an early call-and-response pattern mode, hand clapping, memorable rhythms, and vocal harmonization. However, as it became widespread, the band's sound became prominent. Soul music relied on the improvisational skills of their musicians, and in the end, it was the band that provided the sound that became part of soul music. It is within this historic and social context that soul music came into being.

---

[15] http://www.pbs.org/wnet/americanmasters/sister-rosetta-tharpe-full-episode/2516/

Norah Jones   Rosetta Tharpe on guitar

Today, it's impossible to distinguish black and non-black soulful entertainers if you have never seen them. The legacy that non-African American singers have left on R&B is noteworthy, and it is still growing. Rhythm and blues has captured the hearts and minds of so many people, past and present. Female white soulful divas of the past like Chris Clark or Debbie Dean or contemporary artists like Norah Jones or Teena Marie, show that good music has no color. Male and female Latino artists of the past, like Ralfi Pagan or Afro-Filipino Joe Batan, can stir up some soulful sounds. Vocal Latin groups like Voice of Theory or Sweet Sensation are up there competing for a piece of the pie. Italian soulful singers of the 1960s like Timi Yuro, displays the heartfelt songs coming from deep within her being. Also, Michael McDonald impresses his audience with his soulful slow jamming style of singing. Then we have Elliot Yamin, Robin Thicke, and too many others to mention who have contributed to rhythm and blues. The list goes on, but these artists have soul, and many of them began by singing acappella. We should be grateful that these people and many other entertainers like them love and respect the music we call variety of names today. Some call it R&B, soul, doo-wop, or blue-eyed soul. The main thing to remember is that singers, songwriters, record producers, and show promoters all played a part in promoting the beautiful music that we call nowadays rhythm and blues. It is within this setting that performers created a fusion groove, and that groove is growing and influencing millions of people. What happened was the birth of a new sound and this new music became a new genre.

THE GENTRIFICATION OF RHYTHM AND BLUES

The term *gentrification* is the process of urban middle- or upper-class families moving into low-income communities and changing the character of the neighborhood. The end result is the fixing up of old building, homes, starting new businesses and raising the standard of living within the community. In some cases, the poor must move out. In this section, the term will be employed in a broad sweeping manner as a metaphor for the changes that have taken place in the genre we call doo-wop or street corner singing. In 1963, when there was an explosion of young talent along the acappella corridor (Boston-Philadelphia) on the East Coast, the vocal group harmony landscape significantly changed into a multi-ethnic/racial brand. The change has not abated and it continues to grow and expand and, unfortunately, it forced the original founders of the music—black folks—to reconsider their musical position: "I'm on the outside looking in". This change was not intentional on the part of non-African Americans, but a result of economic and social conditions that were happening during that period. In truth, the miscegenation of black singers with white vocalists began with the blues music which bred a "mulatto music" complexion in the 1920s.

In other words, white singers vaulted into the black music arena and started to sing the blues. This socially illegal spontaneous marriage of black and white entertainers set the stage for the present gentrification of black music we have now. White blues singers of the 1920s like Marion Harris set the blueprint and the effects are with us today. In addition to this is as a footnote, Jimmie Rodgers, a country singer was considered then the king of white blues singers.

Blues, jazz, and R&B have become for the most part, a "white-ethnic" assemblage of musicians and singers. Contrary to popular belief, R&B has changed in shades, just like blues and jazz. Its historical roots are in the black experience, but its patrons are white, and a considerable number of entertainers are not black. For example, Wayne Cochran and his CC Riders is a product of that change. Another case in point is jazz, which has a black historical connection, and has now become a genre that has a predominantly large white audience. The same can be said of other musical styles. What was once a genre that was black in origin with a primarily black audience has changed. Perhaps it is due to social-economic changes, or the influx of new immigrants coming to our shores. In either case, the reality is that rhythm and blues has become a different shade in the color spectrum.

Smokey Robinson   Human Nature

One transformation that we see today by way of example in this century is the introduction of the new Detroit-Motown sound. Today a new generation of non-African Americans, whose grandparents fifty years ago were "dancing in the street", is now enjoying it. A case in point is Human Nature, a Caucasian vocal group from Australia produced by the legendary Motown soulful singer Smokey Robinson. Black folks are scratching their heads in bewilderment and seeing "white guys" singing like soulful black entertainers. In reality, it is a testimony to the enduring black sound that so many non-African American people love and appreciate. But how did this gentrification take place and what led to this appeal of black music to a non-black populace? Perhaps the answer to this can be found by going back into the past with the birth of rock 'n' roll and beyond. Rock 'n' roll had its birth in the 1950s, and from there we can trace back the umbilical cord of group singing to the 1930s and 1940s with groups like the Ink Spots and the Mills Brothers.

The musical style of singing of the late 1940s and early 1950s with groups like The Ravens, Sonny Til & the Orioles, and many others had an impact on the birth of rock 'n' roll. There is an overlapping of black performers within this time period and before were singing gospel hymns from 1930–50, like The Dixie Humming Birds or The Golden Gate Quartet. All of these singing groups in some fashion sculpted what we now call rock 'n' roll and, accurately, the "group sound". However, the classic group sound, which we now call doo-wop, and the era in which it was sung, 1955-1959, began to transform itself. The group sound changed away from black and a partly mixed group of entertainers into a multi-ethnic mix in the 1960s with the birth of the new urban acappella pop genre. Keep in mind that there were multi-racial ethnic vocal groups during the 1950s, but the transformation was more prominent as a class during the 1960s.

When the birth of acappella began in 1960s, it was a continuation of the vocal group style of the 1950s. This time period is frequently called the "Golden Age of Acappella", a term used by Jerry Wexler of Atlantic Records as a disparaging remark when groups had to sing without music in his studio for lack of musician availability. Fileti writes:

"If industry pros like Atlantic's Jerry Wexler subtly mocked the so-called "Golden Age of Acappella" (his words), it was because of the off-key and poorly recorded singles, which appealed to many young group harmony fans in the early sixties".[16]

---

[16] http://lulusko.www7.50megs.com/TIMESSQUARE/tsr2.htm

The Larkings   Marion Harris

The transformation that was taking place along the acappella corridor during the 1960s social-cultural upheaval in urban cities was an unanticipated mix of racial-ethnic teenagers coming together. These teenagers recreated their own versions of their favorite "cover songs" from the 1950s. The new vocal group sound was no longer black groups singing songs of the past decades, but non-African Americans singing, promoting, and preserving the black sound of the 1950s. Thus, we have in the mid-1970s and beyond "white groups" doing what black groups did twenty years prior. The musical sway of group harmony flowed from the original pioneer acappella artists of the 1960s through the 1970s and has continued into the music of today. The makeover and transformation was complete; doo-wop became a gentrified genre of black music sung mostly by a mixed ethnic-racial assemblage.

What has happened during the past fifty years since the birth of acappella as a new urban pop genre is a sub-musical culture and cottage industry which has sprung up within the confines of rhythm and blues. This self-contained musical expression, within a small body of vocal group aficionados, is primarily non-African American. It has also become a "regional-centric" category despite the fact that it is sung and heard in Spain, England, Germany, Japan, Australia, and many other countries. Yet it is still known as an East Coast urban musical style of singing. Like gentrification in urban cities, blacks have moved out of their musical neighborhood. Many within the African-American community have not taken advantage of capitalizing on this profitable industry. Smokey Robinson of Motown, for example, capitalized on the sound that Berry Gordy created is re-introducing black music to a primarily young white audience by white entertainers. Introducing white groups is not new; The Valadiers became the first Caucasian vocal group on the Motown label, when they recorded *"Greetings, This Is Uncle Sam"* in 1961. As a footnote, when they first auditioned as a group, it was a racially mixed group or U.N. group. Gordy said to the group, go home, and come back as one color. He wanted a group that was of one racial or ethnic background. In the end, this vocal group came back as one color, and demonstrated that non-black groups with soul can attract all kinds of people.[17] This has not happened in the black community with doo-wop.

---

[17] Phone conversion with Stuart Avig original member of The Valadiers.

The impetus for this goes back over fifty years, beginning during the 1960s when the social, cultural, and musical upheaval was transforming the sound of music in urban America. African Americans were in the process of creating new sounds and discarding the old or renovating something antiquated and making it new: Soul. Now, some African Americans are asking questions—why this is happening? Many black Americans in the music business are not involved in the doo-wop industry, but their counterparts are. Most disc jockeys who play oldies or promote vocal group rhythm and blues are primarily white. Those who produce doo-wop shows are non-African Americans like TJ Lubinsky, Cool Bobby B, Jerry Blavat, or the late Richard Nader. The overwhelming majority of people who go to see doo-wop, classic R&B, or oldies shows are Caucasian. Even doo-wop organizations like the former United Group Harmony Association out of Clifton, New Jersey, was largely a white association of members who loved the black vocal group sound. The Vocal Group Harmony Association from New Jersey, which has replaced U.G.H.A, meets regularly and sponsors events to keep the music alive. Most members are mostly white/ethnic and come together to sing. All this leads us to believe that black music is worth preserving and it does not matter what skin color or ethnic background a person may be. Nevertheless, it does pose some hard questions. Some within the African-American community are saying silently, "These white guys are making money on our music". Others are saying, "They stole our music". Perhaps, but Bob Davis of Soul-Patrol.com, an educator and radio host, says it best:

"Black Americans tend to create a great culture and then throw it away. Black Americans get mad when other people take the culture they no longer seem to want and then start making money from it".[18]

All this leaves us with some questions that we must face in light of what is developing within the vocal group/doo-wop genre. Will this genre remain a sustainable musical style or will it lose its historic black connection? Dr. Charles and Pamela Horner, non-African Americans and doyens of rhythm and blues are doing their best to educate the public about the history of rhythm and blues and vocal group harmony singing. Dr. Horner conducts workshops and seminars educating the public and institutions about the importance of preserving the vocal group sound of black artists. Teaching and promoting the roots of black vocal group harmonization is of great importance. Like gentrification, black folks are missing their historical past and are almost forced to move out of the way for new soulful white singers who have no real connection to the past. This is not wrong in itself, but this is what is happening. This is also going on in blues and jazz. Blues has also become a gentrified musical genre with an audience that is mostly white and includes a large

---

[18] http://www.soul-patrol.com/soul/doowop.html

number of players who are also Caucasians. This can be seen in the yearly Chicago Blues Festival held during the summer. The changing of color in music does not end with jazz, and blues; R&B has changed its entire complexion. Non-African American singers and supporters have a fascination with black music and romanticize it. Many do not understand the social and historical components that make up rhythm and blues. White audiences viewing a black group sing or a blues player play in a large showplace is not the same as seeing them in a small black club in Newark or small black hamlet in Mississippi. Whites would not venture into a black community for fear they may be a target for crime. That is why during the 1950s and 1960s, rock 'n' roll shows like Alan Freed or Murray the K were held in neutral mixed communities. Most white teenagers gravitated to the Brooklyn Paramount rather than to the Apollo Theater in Harlem because the multitude was a mixed ethnic-racial crowd.

The bottom line to gentrification in music is that it is a social-cultural undertaking or phenomenon that moves freely like a spirit in various camps. If there are those who are concerned that rhythm and blues might be losing its historical roots, then participation in educating the public should be encouraged. If the black populace is concerned, then they should reexamine their roots and promote the roots of black music. On the other hand, the black community must not discriminate against their white counterparts who love their music.

A case in point is in 1989, when soulful white singer George Michael won the R&B American Music Award for best album, Faith. There was an undercurrent of protest and criticism against him by some within the black community. It was racial and not based on his ability and talent as a dynamic singer. The black community does not need "white folks" to do it for them, but the reality is, non-blacks to some degree, are keeping the music alive. Nowadays, it appears that there are more educators, promoters, and writers who are non-African American who are engaged in teaching, writing and promoting vocal group harmonization than there are blacks. This should make the black community aware that something is amiss. If African Americans feel that they are losing their cultural musical heritage, then something must be done about it. However, Bob Davis of Soul Patrol.com has been educating the public, both black and white, for years about the history of black music in general. As an educator, Davis has lifted the taboos and speaks straight to the heart. His no-nonsense approach, without political correctness, speaks the truth to his radio audience. Davis is one of the leading spokespeople in the U.S. who speaks about the history of black music. His warm, transparent, and candid approach on the radio gives him the voice to proclaim what is going on in urban America musically. Non-African Americans are only doing what they love and that is promoting R&B group singing. In truth, music belongs to everyone. If the music is beautiful and uplifting with rich harmonies, it belongs to all of us.

Bob Davis

Soul-Patrol.com

Jerry Blavat (Courtesy http://thekey.xpn.org/)

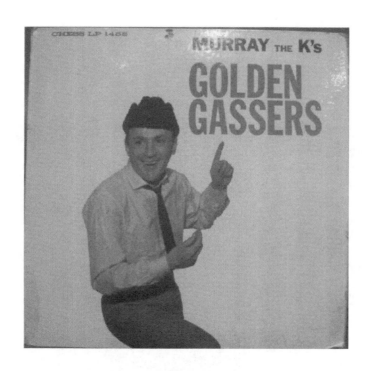

Brooklyn Paramount

Dr. Charles and Pam Horner with Val and Patty Shively

(Shively archives)

Dick Clark (Dick Clark archives)

(Bob King archives)

Teenarama (Circa 1960s Bob King archives)

American Bandstand (Courtesy
http://theprincesandprincessesofdance.com/)

3

DEBUNKING THE PROFESSIONAL MYTH

"Those who do not know their opponent's arguments do not completely understand their own."

During the 1960s, rhythm and blues vocal group singing from the 1950s era was preserved and promoted by acappella artists. Hundreds of vocal groups, many of them mostly teenagers, covered the acappella corridor of urban America. The black-owned magazine, Ebony from Chicago, in 1956 reported that two hundred rock 'n' roll vocal groups were affirming their youth followers with their songs. These teenage vocal groups were doing what they knew best, connecting emotionally in song and affirming their right to be heard. Occasionally, however, the term amateur, when used in a conversation among music aficionados, sometimes comes across as a disparaging comment. It is used most often in context, when referring to an acappella artist as it relates to the 1960s. It is used when they are comparing acappella vocal groups of the 1960s with groups that came a decade or two later, but on no occasion is it used a decade before the 1960s. Unfortunately, it is always the same line of reasoning in the mind of some of vocal group aficionados. Vocal group performers who sang acappella during the 1960s were just amateurs who sang for fun; they were inexperienced, and they were young. Here, we have a prevaricate state of mind. Almost all acappella performers wanted very much to sing professionally and make a living out of it. It was their chance to make it in the real world of music despite their youth. The fact is, the vast majority of vocal group performers who sang and recorded in the late 1940 and into the

1950s were amateurs. Rhythm and blues historian and author, Marv Goldberg, said the following:

"I would agree that most groups were "amateur"... but in the free-for-all of the 50s, most groups formed while in school and thus couldn't be full-time singers even if they wanted to".[19]

This is part of the misinformation myth to demean the 1960s acappella era as insignificant. This canard, and those who espouse this mantra, attempts to re-create the acappella era to fit into a different historical timeline, or no timeline at all. However, more than that, they want to establish that the real decade of acappella began during the 1980s and up into the early 1990s. Let us start with the definition of an amateur so we can see what it means in context before we go any further. By definition, amateur is a noun, a person who engages in a pursuit, especially on an unpaid basis. Synonyms: non-professional, non-specialist, layman, layperson. Adjective-engaging or engaged in without payment; non-professional.

The above definition clearly refers to someone who is involved in an activity or interest without being paid. Let us begin with vocal groups of the 1950s, who for the most part never received any compensation for many of their recordings. Some recorded for major labels, others recorded on independent labels, and still others on subsidiaries. Many vocal groups of the 1950s were never paid, and the vast majority were not professional by definition; they were all amateurs. A large number of high school students made commercial recordings; however, a minuscule number of vocal groups from the 1950s made a

---

[19] Santiago, Abraham J. "Re: Vocal Groups." Message to Marv Goldberg. 27 December 2014. E-mail.

living out of singing. The vast majority of singing groups was in school or had full-time jobs supporting their families.

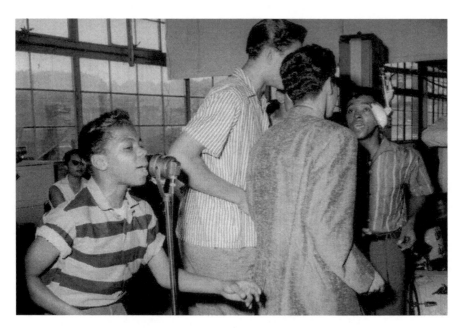

Frankie Lymon and The Teenagers

From the standpoint of defining amateur, the groups of the 1950s were non-professional enthusiasts. If we are going to be consistent with labeling and categorizing groups, then we should not single out acappella performers and categorize them as amateurs, unless we call the 1950s groups amateurs too. Second, some use the same moniker, amateur, to indicate recordings made. Many vocal groups from the 1950s made few recordings, and some made substantial recordings. If the number of recordings made is the criteria for being a professional, then we have a problem. A large number of acappella performers made a considerable amount of records in a short period. There were many groups from the 1950s that made only a single or two and yet some music buffs call them professionals. Third, some refer to the term amateur by the way they sang, and the way they carried themselves on stage. Keep in mind that an acappella artist sang raw with no band or instruments to cover their vocal flaws, if any. It takes more talent to be on pitch, be on the right note, and blend with other voices without a band to cover mistakes. Groups then never used a pitch pipe on stage just before they are going to sing as many do today. Groups of the 1960s memorized their notes and were on key before they sang. Unfortunately, many of those who hold to this position were not there in person when they sang; all they have is a recording and the same can be said of 1950s artists.

Lastly, some use the term amateur to indicate "color" because these groups were predominately non-African Americans. In other words, only "vocal groups of color" who sang during the 1950s are considered professionals. Performers who sang during the acappella era were not, for the most part, people of color, and since they are not, they are considered non-professionals. Here we have "race" as a criteria used to determine a professional group. This double standard is used for one historical period in contrast to the acappella era. Critics should not refer to the acappella age as an amateur time period unless they acknowledge the 1950s era.

The vast majority of groups during the 1950s and 1960s never made a living singing. Classic examples are The Chords who hail from the Bronx. They started singing in high school like most acappella groups, made commercial recordings that received airtime, sold their 45s in record shops, and appeared in public venues. Despite their release of records, they were amateurs because they were still in high school and did not eke out a living from it. Another example is the Five C's out of Gary, Indiana; they all worked full-time jobs in the steel mills. Their gigs were on weekends like most amateur group performers. The list of vocal groups from the 50s who did not make a full-time living from singing is extensive. Vocal groups of the 1950s share the same historical background as the acappella artist. The vast majority were in school or had jobs supporting their families. In regards to the decades that followed the 1960s, the vast majority were also non-professional singers. They also had full-time jobs supporting their families.

Their singing acts happened on weekends or whenever they could come together and do a gig. Now to the present, an example of not being paid is illustrated in the group, The Dells. In the documentary film about the Dells, Marvin Junior complained of not being paid and the hardships they went through in their early career.[20] Also by way of another example, Jerry Lawson, lead singer of The Persuasions said his group still has not been rightfully paid after 20 albums, and singing with his group for forty years. This mindset was very typical of that period, and today many artists still have not received royalties due to them.

---

[20] https://www.youtube.com/watch?v=tX_EU2OI6CA

The Dells

In the end, teens who sang during the 1950s and 1960s carved a new identity in the R&B family of vocal group singing. An argument could possibly be made that they were "quasi-professional", but only in the sense that they made commercial recordings.

Another argument could be made that their recordings were played on the radio; their records were bought in records shops, and they sang in venues wherever they could get in and pass for adults. In reality, acappella groups were not paid and the same goes for groups of the 50s, and that is the basis for being a professional. Despite their youth, they managed to shape and carve a distinctive sound that brought legions of young people to hear and enjoy their music. They broke the barrier of race music, and in the end, their vocal style has continued to grow and it has not abated.

The Royal Counts with Stan Krause

The Original Mixed Company

Louaries

Uniques

THE HUDSON SOUND

During the 1960s, music became a medium of expressing social conditions of the time as well as conveying a different musical style. The music of the 1960s, for the most part, was part urban, regional, country, and a little bit of everything in between. Musicians and singers were venting frustration, spirituality, sex, love, and peace. One could say it was a time when music was simultaneously experimental and creative. As a matter of fact, this time was probably the most creative in the history of American music. The musical culture even created a distinct style of dress and behavior depending on which brand one gravitated to. All of this demonstrated the power of both music and singers, who sought to lift the mundane life of their listeners to something more meaningful and purposeful. Perhaps one of the best examples is found in Psychedelic Rock, which became popular during the mid-1960s with its own sound, cultural ethos, art, and fashion style. Psychedelic Rock was a hippie counter-culture musical style that expressed itself with the use of hallucinogenic drugs and other mind-educing chemicals. San Francisco, California was the breeding ground and became a focal point for young people who believed they could make a difference by playing music and getting high. The vocal band, Cream, with their hit "White Room" is an obvious example of the psychedelic sound. Smith writes:

"Although critics dismissed the psychedelic music of this period as being too loud, too experimental, and, most worryingly, too tied up with the emerging drugs and the drug culture, critic and historian, Sheila Whiteley, contends that psychedelic music was characterized both by its complexity and its paradoxes. While psychedelic music was closely

aligned with the drugs and the drug culture—and may, in some ways, be understood as a product of that subculture—it was still, like folk music, a genre of protest, but it was a specific form of protest distinct from the lyrically imperative folk music".[21]

---

[21] articlemyriad.com/influence-60s-psychedelic-music-culture-modern-society

In contrast to the Psychedelic Rock sound of San Francisco is the Motown sound of Detroit, Michigan. The Motown sound produced sharp, well-groomed, and disciplined singers and musicians. The Funk Brothers Band of Motown was, in essence, the power behind Motown's success, and produced hit after hit from an urban regional sound to a more nationwide and international sound. The Motown writers (Holland, Dozier and Holland) with the help of the Funk Brothers, became the sound of young America and were often portrayed as such to the public. There were other regional sounds like the Memphis sound Stax Records with its raw, gritty, soulful sound capturing the emotion of the singer and transferring that sound to the listener. Singers and musicians communicated all of the above musical styles with the heartfelt sounds of life. Nevertheless, one regional sound emerged within this multi-faceted mix of music from the 1960s; this sound was unique from all the other competing musical forms. It was different; and unlike any other musical genre or sound ever produced, it was the Hudson Sound. What is the Hudson Sound?

The Funk Brothers of Motown

Jersey City 1960s

Jersey City and New York City on the Hudson today

The Hudson Sound is acappella vocal group singing, a distinctive style that was born on the banks of the Hudson River where New York and New Jersey meet. It is a unique singing style and class that is represented by seven essential elements. These seven distinct markings or components make the Hudson Sound unique.

First, singing was done acappella in an aural harmonic fashion. Prior to the birth of acappella in 1963 as a new pop genre, there were no commercial industry recording singers who sang strictly acappella.

Second, the Hudson Sound was a meeting of the twains. It was a fusion of two different assemblages of vocal styles from two different communities on both sides of the Hudson River: New York and New Jersey.

Third, it was a tenor sound, as opposed to the soulful-indigo style of music that was coming out of places like Memphis, Detroit, or Muscle Shoals.

Fourthly, the musical vocals were sung mostly by non-African Americans who were brought up and nurtured on rhythm and blues.

Fifthly, it was a male dominated cluster of vocal groups with almost no females represented.

Sixth, the Hudson Sound was a group act of quintets and quartets. There were no solo acts where individuals sang acappella on stage or made solo acappella recordings.

And seven, the Hudson Sound was never claimed or owned by a record label like Motown Records or Stax Records which promoted their distinct sound; no record label proclaimed the Hudson Sound as their own.

However, before we begin discussing the Hudson Sound, first it is important that we again define acappella and how it is used today compared to how it was used fifty plus years ago in urban America. Acappella is an Italian word, as was mentioned earlier, which means 'in the style of the chapel'. It is usually identified as choral or ensemble singing without musical instrumentation within a sacred-religious setting. Today, as it is used, it has more of generic meaning to the original definition. Colleges and universities all have some type of small-to-large acappella chorales. Music organizations, associations, and clubs have acappella singers. With that said, we need to re-define what it meant fifty years ago in the inner cities of America. When this word was first coined by Irving Slim Rose owner of Times Square Records in New York City fifty years ago, it meant vocal group harmonization in the rhythm and blues style. It did not mean anything else. Since acappella singing is performed without a band or orchestra, the focus is always on the singers.

The concentration was always on blending voices or harmonizing with each singer. Vocal groups had a lead singer, a first or second tenor, a baritone, and a bass. Some vocal groups may have had a female lead singer like the Heartaches; but generally speaking, it was a male group consisting of four or five men. With this said, let us explore the claim that a new sound emerged during the 1960s.

Let us begin with the most obvious; the Hudson Sound is acappella in its primitive harmonic language. Acappella became the new urban neighborhood art form of the 1960s.

There were no bands or instrumental ensembles to cover or fill in vocal flaws. Singers would listen to the audio recording (45s) and learned their parts.

They had no music sheet to read from; they all learned their parts in an aural harmonic fashion. Singers did not use vocal gymnastics like beat boxing, vocal chopping, or other vocal maneuvers to create a sound that resembles an instrument as we have today. Groups sang raw as best they could. The simple triads and basic harmonic chords made the Hudson Sound unique. The acappella pioneers introduced a new commercial venture in the music recording business. For the first time in American music history, independent record companies were started specifically for the purpose of recording acappella artists for commercial use. This was never done before in music history. An acappella industry emerged and became a niche within the corporate music sphere. Major record companies like Atlantic, Mercury, and others viewed acappella as an unprofitable business venture and not worthy of consideration. It was considered then, and now, a black sheep within the music industry. This whole concept of producing and recording singers to sing without a band or orchestra was out-of-the-box thinking. For the young pioneers who started this new genre, it proved to be very profitable. In the end, major record labels missed out on what could have been a gold mine of talent and money if only they had the courage to think outside of the box. The real losers in this new, untapped enterprise were the major record companies. These companies failed to hear the voices of neighborhood young people and respond to a new sound.

The second distinguishing mark of the Hudson Sound was that it was a fusion of two major communities: New York and New Jersey. It was a fusion of two distinct sounds coming from the five boroughs of New York City and across the river Jersey City and its neighboring communities. The coming together of two communities from both sides of the Hudson River and along the acappella corridor that stretched from Boston to Philadelphia-Pittsburg area became a distinctive sound. Acappella was the social glue that cemented cities and neighborhoods together. It was the unforgettable intros, the magical harmonies, and the soaring vocals that made the sound distinctive. There was an urban musical syncretism that provided a unity within a diverse community of singers and ethnic backgrounds. Both localities developed their own particular vocal style and linguistic flair that meshed into a new sound. It was not intentional, but a process of assimilating with one another and producing something different.

Thirdly, the Hudson Sound was a tenor sound as opposed to the soulful, gritty sound that was emanating from Detroit and Memphis. When we compare the Hudson Sound to the unwavering soulful sound coming from Motown or other regions like Muscle Shoals, Alabama where Wilson Picket flourished, we get a sense of how different and unique the sound was. It is unique not only because it was sung in acappella, but in how this was achieved. The Hudson Sound is perhaps reminiscent of the style of singing that existed during the 1920s, 30s, and 40s. when tenor singers dominated the theatrical and musical venues of that period. Then, the scene changed with the appearance of a singer by the name of Bing Crosby who changed the landscape of pop singing by introducing a mellow, rich baritone sound to the public arena. His voice influenced the public perception that baritones have a place in the musical field alongside tenors. Friedwald comments:

"Crosby is the biggest influence on American popular singing. Before Bing there was no baritone in the popular field only tenors. Crosby made America baritone-conscious and popularized the rich deep tones that move people so much. Crosby revolutionized modern singing. Crosby achieved all this largely from his own absorption of black style, and served a function of such importance to the development of Afro-American vocal music partly because he returned to blacks what was rightfully theirs".[22]

---

[22] Friedwald, W. Jazz Singing: America's Great Voices From Bessie Smith To Bebop And Beyond. New York: Da Capo Press. (1990). Pg.252

The acappella era re-introduced, in a historical cyclic fashion, the tenor vocal range of singing. Not all who sang acappella during this period had sky-high harmonies or prominent tenors. However, if we were to give a broad sweeping general view of the many groups represented during this time, we can probably say that a good percentage had high tenors within their groups. But then again, it would not be what we call today a mellow baritone or soulful singing scale. Now, there are exceptions, but generally speaking, the Hudson Sound was a tenor scale. There are exceptions in groups like The Persuasions, which would be considered to have a "soulful" baritone range. Vocal groups like The Royal Counts, Notations, and The Chessmen and others are examples of soulful singers. These groups at that time were able to reach the tenor scale effortlessly.

By way of illustration, The Royal Counts produced an LP album entitled "Acappella Soul" in the mid-1960s, and had all the features of using falsetto and the gritty, soulful sound. However, as we review acappella groups of the 1960s, we can say that they represented the finest of non-African American singing groups who did not pretend to be soulful. They sang their own interpretation of material their own way. Their musical repertoire included everything from current hits of the time to Broadway tunes. Examples of prominent vocal groups that exercised tenor ranges are The Rue-Teens, Shadows (aka Five Jades), Autumns, Savoys, and Heartaches. It is important to understand that the tenor scale of singing among acappella vocal groups resurfaced in the 1960s for no apparent reason. The influence of some groups from the 1950s, like Little Anthony and the Imperials, Ronnie, and the Highlights, or groups like The Jive Five may have had a subliminal impact on urban teenagers or groups like them. The main point is that urban teenagers, mostly non-African Americans, sang knowing that they did not have that mellow, low range-gritty style that was shaping American music within rhythm and blues. When soul came on the scene in the early 1960s, it changed and awakened the public to a new sound within the R&B family. What is interesting is that the Hudson Sound was competing with soul and many other musical art forms.

Fourthly, as was mentioned above in passing, the singers who sang acappella were mostly non-African Americans. The vocal adaptations and vocal alterations by ethnic groups like Italians, Jewish, and Puerto Ricans allowed them to maintain the heritage of three and four-part harmony rhythm and blues style. These young singers were raised and nurtured on rhythm and blues. Their mentors were groups like The Harptones, Ravens, Swallows, Crests, Five Keys, and many more. Young teenagers went to live shows at the Brooklyn Paramount, Apollo Theatre, and various shows in New Jersey. Teenagers listened to disc jockey radio personalities like Alan Freed, Jocko, Cousin Brucie, and Murray the K. In reality, they were immersed in the black music sound of vocal groups.

Fifth, it was truly a male-dominated genre with testosterone flowing like musical chords. Female vocal groups were scarce and girl groups did not venture out to sing on street corners or look for that elusive echo that so many male groups were looking for. One could say it was a narrow-minded assembly of guys who believed that girls belonged at home or in school, not in the street hanging out, trying to hit a few tunes. For young men to observe a group of girls attempting to sing on a street corner was considered culturally and socially unacceptable.

Sixth, the Hudson Sound was a group act; there was no such thing as a solo artist or duets singing acappella and making recordings. The groups who performed were usually quintets, quartets, and generally all male. When groups performed on stage, their dance routines were simple, reflecting the song being sung. It was in this historical and social context, that the Hudson Sound stood out among other regional musical sounds of the 1960s.

Lastly, the Hudson Sound was never under one particular record label or umbrella, like Motown Records and their subsidiaries, or Memphis under Stax Records. The Hudson Sound was being promoted by many independent acappella record labels, all of them promoting raw, unadulterated street corner singing. Keep in mind that the acappella record labels were owned by non-African Americans males, all under twenty-five years of age. These seven distinctions made the Hudson Sound unique and led it to become the very first urban, vocal musical style to appear on the American scene way before hip hop or rap.

To summarize this briefly in a sentence or two, the musical styles of the 1960s included the Hudson Sound which was in the forefront, competing with the pioneering Funk-Soul of James Brown, Motown, and Blues-Rock-jazz blend of Jimi Hendrix, Surfing Sound of the Beach Boys, British Sound, Muscle Shoals, Country, Folk, and many others. All the musical genres of the 1960s, from folk music to Latin Soul, were all competing with one another and the Hudson Sound was right there in the midst of the big musical sounds. Acappella vocal groups and their pioneers did something that no other genre ever did. They carved out a new sound within the rhythm and blues genre, and created a new record industry. The Hudson Sound became the very first genus within rhythm and blues, whose singers were primarily non-African-Americans. When we compare the uniqueness of the Hudson Sound with their fusion of two distinct localities, their soaring tenors, and their singing in acappella, we have a sound that was different, unusual, and strictly an urban neighborhood sound of the city.

New York City on the Hudson River

The Notations

The Royal Counts

Savoys

Don Fileti & Val Shively

(Val Shively archives)

Unknown vocal group from Harlem in Bobby's record shop

Bobby Robinson in front of his store in Harlem

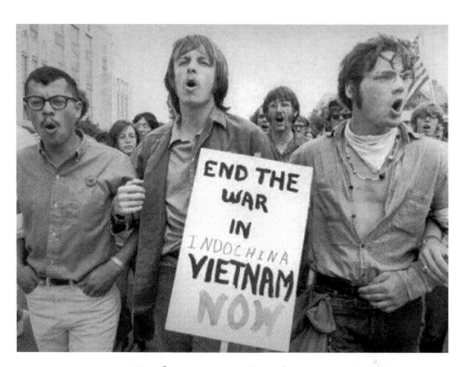

Students protesting the war

(https://apush-wiki-marlborough-school.wikispaces.com)

4

GERIATRIC SINGERS

"We may be old, but we still got it."

It was a cool summer night on the Hudson River facing Lower Manhattan. On the Jersey City side, guys were all huddling together on the dock. Lady Liberty was glancing at the skyline as guys began to sing in four-part harmony. The song that they were singing was recorded a few years back by The Valadiers, *"Greetings, this is Uncle Sam"*. The year was 1966; Vietnam was calling young men to the war in Asia. These guys, young and full of energy, would have to serve Uncle Sam in some capacity or face the consequences. For four years, they formed a bond, a deep connection rooted in friendship and music. Now that union may very well be in jeopardy because of the looming war before them. What will happen to them? Will they return to their old neighborhood in which they grew up? Will they continue to sing after the war is over? This story was repeated many times over. Today those same guys who once sang on the waterfront are now aging senior citizens with memories of the past echoing, prompting them to sing again. They are still harmonizing and singing those tunes, perhaps not as clean and crisp as when they were in their teens, but they're still able to convey a song in a meaningful and mellow way. Here lies the problem; how does a senior citizen express his love for group harmony singing to a generation that knows nothing about the vocal group R&B genre called doo-wop?

One problem that consistently remains unanswered within the vocal group harmonization genre is the inability to clearly communicate the music to a new and younger generation. Currently, the vast majority of R&B acappella singers and those who attend doo-wop shows are senior citizens. Vocal group clubs and venues that exist today look more like geriatric singers who are living in their past glory. This in itself is one of the problems with the current vocal group genre. Vocal group enthusiasts have failed to pass on what they love to a new, young generation. As of today, there are few young vocal group singers for young people to emulate. There are very few, if any, youthful doo-wop groups between the ages of fifteen to twenty-eight years of age. There are no youthful R&B acappella groups who are on Billboard magazine charts or who are being showcased to a young audience. The average age of group singers who came out of the 1960s era are sixty-eight to seventy-three, and this age group does not attract young people to their cause. The lack of current young doo-wop vocal groups in the music world today, is evidence of their failure to communicate their music. The problem not only lies with doo-wop aficionados who sing, but also with clubs who sponsor them and radio personalities. There are exceptions like the up and coming group Whiptones however, there are not many more that are being showcased.

The formations of social singing clubs are all in the same boat. Groups who come together to connect and sing are old. These groups are simply senior citizens, and this is not appealing to youth. In an email comment, Wayne Stierle confirms that the young are not interested:

"The only ones who care about this music, for the most part, are about fifty years old and older".[23]

The stark reality is even fifty-year-old's do not listen to this genre that much. The exact age is between sixty-five and seventy years of age who continue to sing, and who goes to oldies shows. Not only is it not appealing to young people, but it does not advance their goal. These group members are islands unto themselves. Their musical mindset is narrow. Their repertoire consists of songs from the '50s and early '60s. For this reason, the Godfather of acappella, Jerry Lawson, refuses to be pegged as a doo-wop vocalist or as part of a doo-wop vocal group when he sang with the Persuasions. He would rather be called a soul singer/R&B pop singer than be pegged as a doo-wop singer. Few, if any, would venture to sing songs by contemporary artists or songs by Bobby Womack or Barry White. Most, if not all, of them would not dare to sing any songs by current R&B singers. Most do not even know who the current R&B singers are, let alone know any present-day songs. A geriatric group member, if asked whether he knows Joss Stone, Robin Thicke, or Amy Winehouse, would draw a blank, and the blank stare would not be dementia, though it could very well be.

---

[23] Santiago, Abraham J. Message to Wayne Stierle June 2013. Email.

Remember Then

Another problem facing the vocal group genre is that it has remained a regional white-centric genre within a subculture of R&B music. Non-blacks have taken the R&B vocal group sound and have made it their own since the early '60s. Most "oldies doo-wop shows" featuring groups of the 1950s and '60s have very few African-Americans in their audience. The cottage industry of doo-wop is non-African-American, and promoters like T.J. Lubinsky, and classic doo-wop disc jockeys are generally non-African-Americans. This adds to the perception that this genre is ethno regional-centric. The region that provides the most impetus to the genre is the Atlantic Coast from Boston to the Pittsburgh-Philadelphia area, the acappella corridor. There is no real explanation as to why this phenomenon has occurred. Black Americans, as was stated before, prefer something new to something old. It is this old style of group harmonization that may be the reason why black folks are not supporting this genre.

Lastly, non-African-Americans who love the group sound, especially those who are disc jockeys, educators, and concert promoters, have failed, in general, to connect with black leaders in the music industry. There are exceptions, as in all things. Bob Davis has said:

"One of the "myths" in the black community is that black folks who are involved in this type of music are somehow "Uncle Toms." That "myth" somehow implies that because the modern-day audience for the music is about 95% white, that the artists themselves are somehow "sellouts." The reality is that black folks need to be SPANKED for their own ignorance"![24]

Connecting with the urban black neighborhoods in general could be an incentive in providing young people with an alternative lifestyle and introducing them to the classic R&B group sound. Vocal group singing can be an instrument for propelling young people to sing, write songs, and join a music community. Forming partnerships with black radio stations, churches, forming alliances with black-owned business, colleges, and organizations all help in promoting the classic group sound. In summarizing what was mentioned above, here are the three factors that pose the greatest challenges in keeping the group sound from advancing; age, ethnic centered, and not connecting with the black community. Devotees of the R&B group sound can have an impact once they remove

---

[24] http://www.soul-patrol.com/soul/doowop.html

themselves from their myopic mindset. If country music can be played in New York City with a large listenership, there is no reason why classic doo-wop cannot be heard in Moab, Utah. To advance our genre, we need to promote and train young people in our music. One place could be middle schools and high schools forming youth clubs that promote vocal group singing and live shows or talent shows geared towards teenagers. Lastly, the organization Rock 'n' Roll Forever Foundation from New York City is an excellent organization to connect with. They have made it their goal to reach young people with all types of musical genres, and that includes doo-wop.[25]

GIRL GROUPS DURING THE ACAPPELLA YEARS

Male and female vocal groups played a significant role during the rock 'n' roll years of the 1950s and early '60s. However, the role of girl groups during the acappella era was quite different. The role of male groups during the 1950s and '60s was a male-dominated environment. This is not to say that there were not any girl groups. There were girl groups, and many female groups were spectacular. For some reason, girl groups' ethos or spirit did not translate to the acappella age. It just didn't happen. Part of the reason could have been the acappella producers themselves. Many were fixated on producing male groups, but they also had to deal with the immature behavior of many of these young male adults. It was a balancing act of going to the studio, having groups sing, preventing them from getting into arguments, fights, and a host of other things. Having girls in the same studio would have been a disaster for many record producers. During the acappella era, female groups were in

---

[25] http://www.rockandrollforever.org/

short supply and almost non-existent when it came to record releases. There are various reasons for this. One possible reason for the lack of female vocal groups during the acappella period was due in part to the lack of vocal parts for women. Male groups usually consisted of a four-part harmony. A male group would consist of a lead singer, first tenor, second tenor, baritone, and bass. Girl groups, on the other hand, lacked the low range or bass part to create the mellow sound that is so unique to the street corner music. Few girls had a contralto voice in their group. The vast majority of females were soprano, alto, or maybe mezzo-soprano, but that in itself does not mean anything when it comes to singing. This argument from some acappella enthusiasts is weak, but it is being mentioned to give clarity. However, to provide a more balanced view, this position is presented. There were plenty of songs female groups could have sung, from groups and individuals like The Chantels, Supremes, Shirelles, Mary Wells, Shirley Matthews, or Claudine Clark.

Another reason for the lack of female participation was cultural mores, which perhaps is the strongest argument. It was common for many young girls during this time not to venture outside of their own ethnic-centered neighborhoods and mingle with boys. For some unknown reason, female acappella groups did not take off. One possible reason was the change in the cultural and moral climate of very impressionable young women. Young men still adhered to social behaviors and good manners. Young men avoided swearing in front of young women, avoided coarse sexual-orientated speech, and for the most part, were taught at home about basic good manners. Young women were not called 'bitch' or 'hoe' like we have today.

The old world mindset of daughters and sons of immigrants from the "old country" was always paramount socially. There was always a certain amount of respect and restrain for the opposite sex. Since the vast majority of girls were raised within the context of church or religious affiliation, any deviation from a good, wholesome upbringing was considered taboo. Standing on street corners was not considered wholesome or appropriate behavior. If girls wanted to sing, the stipulations for singing had to be within the confines of a building, preferably a church, synagogue setting, or at home. Mostly likely an adult or chaperone of some maturity had to be present. In addition, parents of teenage girls believed that girls had a place in society, and that was preparing to be good wives and mothers. Standing on street corners, subway stations, and singing does not prepare young girls for motherhood. Most of all, girls were not looking for an echo, but for a man.

Ginger & the Adorables

Citadels

Lastly, record producers were more concerned about male groups in general only because they believed that there was enough musical material to go around. The audience preferred male groups, and guys were easy to handle. Young girls were looked upon as fragile and delicate, not tough as today's women are in the music business. The interesting thing about this time period was that girl groups were carving a notch in the world of music. The group The Chantels for example, who recorded on the End label "He's Gone" and "The Plea", was still in high school. Their real success came when they sang "Maybe", which was released in 1958. Girls during the acappella era had a lot of song material to choose from and girl groups to emulate. Yet, few dared to remove themselves from their parental umbrella, or at least partially. Many girls could not persuade their parents to allow them to have a bit of independence. Parents were zoned into their own reality and worldview. It was a struggle for them to let go. If a record producer was interested in recording a girl group, the parents had to give the okay to the producer. Parents did not give their daughters away and leave them in a studio to record with guys whose sexual drive was at an all-time high. Many times at least one parent or family member would accompany girl groups to make sure no hanky-panky was going on. Yet there certainly was an attempt to record female groups, and Wayne Stierle, Stan Krause, and others did their best to seek out female groups who were interested. Ginger and the Adorables were the first female group to record acappella. Stan Krause recorded Candice Crawford, who recorded with the Royal Counts, although her group the Emeralds never made a commercial recording.

Chantels

For the sake of clarity, The McGuire Sisters did sing acappella cuts like *Sincerely and Goodnight Sweetheart,* originally sung by The Moonglows and The Spaniels, but it was generally sung to showcase their ability to sing in harmony before the public.[26]

It is important to note, that some girls were in groups that featured all males, since some girls were not interested in an exclusively girl group. Girl groups tended to quarrel with each other and flirt or get into jealous moods. For some girls,

---

[26] https://www.youtube.com/watch?v=0DvoO80zEkA

singing with a group of young men was a safety net and provided emotional security. Those who did sing were involved in groups like The Candlelites, Citadels, Heartaches, and The Distinctions. Yet in 1973, to be exact, a group by the name of Sweet Honey in the Rock came on the scene and provided a new style of acappella singing that was soulful, spiritual, and Afro-centric. They could sing anything from Motown favorites to gospel and everything in between, but generally speaking, their repertoire sound had a social element to it. Beatrice Johnson Reagon founded this group with four gorgeous women. In the early 1970s, they were the female counterpart to the Persuasions. Although they are an American Grammy Award-winning vocal group, devotees of the R&B doo-wop singing style were not interested in Sweet Honey in the Rock as a female vocal group.

The reason for this is clear; they did not portray the R&B vocal sound of the 1950s and '60s even though they could sing anything with deep soul and tight harmonies. It demonstrated their penchant for a particular style of singing that excluded any group that did not adhere to their specific, narrow singing style. This has continued and will continue because this is what their main interest is. These fans are die hard R&B devotees similar to the Chicago Cubs fans. So in the end, female groups during the acappella era had no significant influence during this period. All we have are a few unreleased demos and a few recordings. Perhaps somewhere stashed away in a basement there may be a reel-to-reel tape of girls singing; until then, we just have to wait.

The Blossoms

The Emeralds

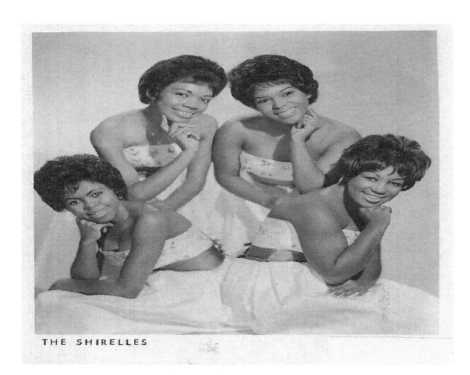

THE SHIRELLES

Sweet Honey in the Rock

Lastly, acappella artists along the Eastern Seaboard were made up of many ethnic groups. As was mentioned previously, these groups were groomed in rhythm and blues. If one was to examine the portfolio of artists, we can safely say that the vast majority of groups who sang and made acappella recordings were not black. If we were to categorize the players within acappella, rock 'n' roll and the background that consisted of singing, songwriting and entrepreneurial empire-building, then we would be bound to consider three main ethnic groups who had a great influence on vocal group harmonization. These ethnic groups are presented here as a springboard for discussion. Each cultural ethnic group overshadowed the rhythm and blues genre in various ways. Keep in mind that the following digest presented here is an overview of these ethnic groups. Let us begin with part two and discover those who played a role in their contribution to R&B.

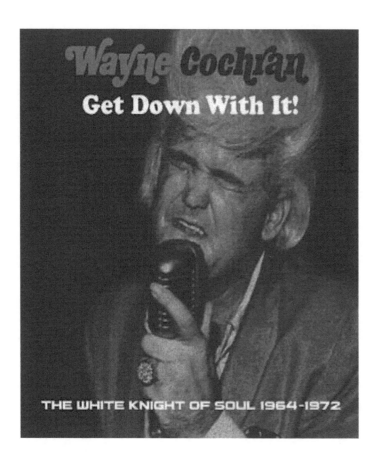

PART TWO

BROTHERS OF ANOTHER SHADE

5

HISPANIC CONTRIBUTION TO RHYTHM AND BLUES

The contribution that Hispanics made to the vocal group harmony scene is widely underestimated and misunderstood. There are few, if any, books on Hispanic contributions to rock 'n' roll, let alone the history of vocal groups. In fact, there is very little written on Hispanic involvement in the vocal groups' scene. Perhaps this is because many Hispanics were in a unique position to play the role of "crossover entertainers". Hispanics were in a crosshair position to straddle the fence on both sides of the racial-ethnic ethos. The reason for this is quite evident. The Hispanic racial composition played a significant role in the development of group singing. The Hispanic racial-type varies widely, from blond hair with blue eyes to black features and everything in between. Because of this makeup, Latinos were comfortable and at home with white ethnic groups as well as black. The term "Hispanic" or "Latino" is used here with a general broad stroke that includes all people whose roots originated from the Iberian Peninsula, the Caribbean, and Latin America.

In the early development of the street corner sound, especially on the Eastern Coast of the United States during the 1950s, Hispanics, primarily Puerto Ricans, were the main vocalists found singing with black and white ethnic groups. They were involved in many of the popular groups. The Crests, featuring Johnny Maestro, included Puerto Ricans. Frankie Lymon and the Teenagers had members who were Puerto Ricans, as did The Tune Weavers. Some groups, like The Claremonts featuring Vince Castro and The Four Haven Knights, had Hispanic members; so did The Cameos featuring the late Victor "Rod" Rodriquez. Other groups that came later, like The Excellents, Devotions, and others, played a pivotal role in shaping the group sound.

On the West Coast, The Jaguars, one of the very first integrated groups commonly referred to as U.N. or interracial groups, had Manny Chavez. Because of their unique position of being able to cross over, some Hispanic vocalists were found in all-white groups and identified as white, usually of Italian descent. Some were associated with black groups, like Juan Gutierrez of The Diablos, and others were viewed as primarily Latinos, like The Eternals. Depending on which area or community Hispanics lived in, some took on the cultural characteristics of the prominent race or ethnic group within the community. Thus, you find some Hispanics gravitating to black culture, Italian culture, Jewish culture or the prominent culture that was within their neighborhood. Regardless of whom they sang and performed with, the Hispanic contribution to the vocal group harmony scene is significant, but understated. Some were involved in managing, recruiting and writing, like Raul Cita of The Harptones, Cliff Martinez of The Crows, Esther Navarro, Cadillacs and Cecilio Rodriguez of The Imperials. Taken as a whole, the part that they played in the vocal group picture is significant. Their participation was vital in uniting and building bridges of understanding along racial and ethnic borders existing in the 1950s and 1960s and helped close the gap between the races. The camaraderie among group members and their friendships spilled over into their performances and had a significant impact on the audience. For this reason, Hispanics helped dispel the concept among white bigots that rock 'n' roll was purely a decadent form of black music. Moreover, many Latinos played a role in the overall development of rock 'n' roll in general.

Puerto Ricans dominated the vocal group scene among Latinos on the Atlantic side. In the Southwest, Mexican-American barrios of Phoenix, Albuquerque, San Antonio and Los Angeles were the scene of Chicano vocal groups, with their soulful rhythm and blues music. "Chicano Soul" was in, and the top groups demonstrated that they could compete with any group as being soulful to the core. Chicano group legends such as The Romancers, The Blendells, and The Premiers were the talk of the town. The most distinguishing characteristic between Puerto Rican street corner crooners on the East Coast, and Chicano brothers in the Southwest is that a guitarist or band behind the vocals, accompanied many Chicano singers. Even in practice sessions, an instrument played a role in the vocals, this was a standard practice.

In contrast, Puerto Ricans on the East Coast held practice sessions in acappella fashion, and generally without musical accompaniment.

Among the noteworthy Chicano groups are The Royal Jesters, with their classic song "My Angel of Love" featuring the late great Dimas Garza, Little Julian Herrera and the Tigers scored hits with "Lonely, Lonely Nights" and "I Remember Linda". Rosie and the Originals, and Ritchie Valens all made a substantial contribution to the vocal group scene and rock 'n' roll. While the 1950s saw the participation of urban Hispanics in the vocal group arena, the acappella explosion of the 1960s was an eruption of Latino talent and participation. Warner writes:

"From 1962 through approximately 1966, an east coast phenomenon occurred in which harmony lovers were brought in contact with hundreds of acappella vocal groups and their recordings created just for that audience".[27]

---

[27] American Singing Groups: A History 1940-1990 Jay Warner – Billboard Book 1992, Pg. 322

CHICANO SOUL:
San Antonio's Westside Sound

SWEET SOUL CHICANO STYLE! 1963-1970

The 1960s gave many urban teenagers of all classes the opportunity to actually record what they had been doing on the street corners and in their bathrooms and building hallways. For the first time, teenagers were able to sing and record their own versions of songs that their favorite groups recorded. All of these teenagers were emulating and continuing the R&B group sound of the 1950s, which had taken a beating as a result of the musical and social changes that were taking place. This opportunity opened the gates for Hispanics not only to be involved in groups that were multiracial, but also to develop their own unique ethnic vocal group style. During the acappella era (1963–1973), a number of solid groups with Hispanic members made a significant contribution; among them were The Five Jades, Chessmen, Zirkons, Concepts, Youngones and Majestics, just to name a few. The acappella era of the 1960s introduced these pioneers and preservers of the group sound. What followed was a movement to record, capture, and continue the rhythm and blues group sound of the 1950s. The role that Hispanics played in forming singing groups helped pave the way in building bridges of understanding between ethnic groups and helped to break the color barrier.

Unfortunately, many historians and vocal group enthusiasts have never investigated the L.A. Chicano vocal group sound or the New York City Latin-Soul group sound. These areas are both open to investigation and study, and stand as one of the major contributions that Hispanics made, not only to vocal group history, but also to rock 'n' roll.

The Five Jades

The Concepts

CHICANO SOUL: TEXAS GROUP TREASURES VOLUME 1

SOUL MUSIC CHICANO STYLE! 1963-1970

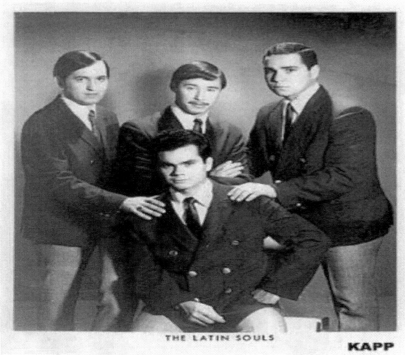

THE LATIN SOULS

KAPP

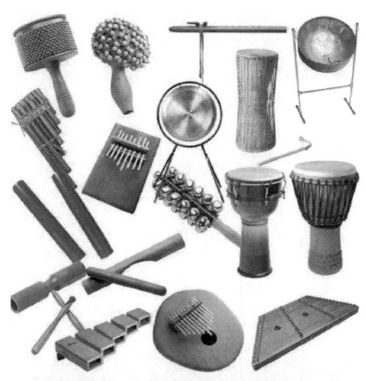

6

ITALIAN CONNECTION TO RHYTHM AND BLUES

In my hometown, Eastchester, New York, there was only one ethnic group who knew everything about rock 'n' roll. They liked loud, flashy colors, and they seemed to have a natural sense of rhythm and an inborn musical ability. They excelled in the school band, and at dances, they cut everybody. They all lived in one section of town, and while it was dangerous to go there after dark, there were a couple of candy stores where they'd sometimes gather to hang out and stand outside and harmonize. My Jewish friends might have had the money to buy the latest rock 'n' roll records, but when it came to swinging it, dancing it, and living the rock 'n' roll life, they had to cross the invisible line into the north end. That's where the Italian kids lived. (You thought I was talking about blacks? Hey, the day the first black moves into that town is the day the last Italian is too weak to fight 'em off.)[28] It is a well-accepted fact

---

[28] http://www.anglistica.unior.it/sites/anglistica/files/05%20Buffa.pdf

that the preservation of the rhythm and blues 1950s vocal group sound is a product of non-African Americans. Davis writes:

"You see; these folks were preservationists of a great culture that Black people no longer seemed to have any use for".[29]

The preservation of the R&B vocal group sound began with street-corner acappella artists in the 1960s along the acappella corridor that stretched from Boston to the Philadelphia-Pittsburg area. These groups were the first and original performers in the preservation of the 1950s black group sound. The credit for the preservation of the rhythm and blues vocal group style goes to Irving Slim Rose of Times Square Records, Stan Krause of Catamount Records and Wayne Stierle of Snowflake Records. Other contributors, including Eddie Grier and Donn Fileti of Relic Records, who valued black singing groups, contributed to the preservation of the group R&B street sound by selling acappella recordings and reissues. It was a combination of all of the above who played a part, and many others like Ralph Nader, Bobby Miller, Gus Gossert and Ronnie I, who were all instrumental in bringing back R&B vocal group singing. To suggest that "only one person" is responsible for the preservation of the group sound is false. The exposure of the 1950s group sound in urban America, which stretched from Boston to Philadelphia-Pittsburgh, influenced various ethnic groups, and the most predominant were Italians. It was the Italian Americans to a large extent who made it fashionable for all "non-black groups" to imitate the black vocal group sound of the 1950s.

---

[29] http://www.soul-patrol.com/soul/doowop.html

Ronnie Italiano, a person who is not well-known in the world of rhythm and blues, had a significant impact in reintroducing discarded 1950s groups back to the stage. Italiano was not a member of a vocal group. His interest was groups in general from the '40s and '50s. Ronnie Italiano started the United Group Harmony Association in the mid-1970s with co-founder Stan Krause of Catamount Records. He launched his new organization with the hope of recovering the old-guard singing groups and having them sing before a public audience. His attempt at starting this association worked, and hundreds of people flocked to see and hear classic groups every month. Not only did he bring back the groups of the past, but he also brought in acappella groups to showcase them before his fans. It was a great success and the old-school groups deeply appreciated what Italiano did for them. His thirty-two years of service in promoting R&B and honoring pioneer singers of the 1940s and 1950s did not go unnoticed. He was instrumental, like others before him, in galvanizing the group sound. He will always be remembered by his fans as a man who loved the rhythm and blues vocal group genre.[30]

When blacks moved from the South to the northern urban areas of the Atlantic coast to find work, they unknowingly influenced musically an ethnic segment of society considerably. It was in this historical-social context that many white teenagers became exposed to the rhythm and blues group sound; in doing so, Italians emerged as the white ethnic symbol in the new and developing group sound genre. It was not until 1957–1958 that

---

[30] Author's note: Wayne Stierle helped launch Ronnie Italiano's career in terms of starting his record label, radio, and other things. E-mail, 25 May 2013

Italian youths began to get out of the adolescent mindset into something better: vocal group singing.

Leading the pack was a Bronx singing group from New York called Dion & the Belmonts. Instead of fighting or getting into rumbles with various ethnic groups like the Irish, Jewish or Puerto Ricans, Italians groups emerged doing battle with their vocal cords. The term "battle of the groups" largely came from the idea of competing with songs rather than competing with fists. Various ethnic groups began to sing and integrate with one another into singing groups. It is within this background, that Italians became known for their high tenor leads and tight, soulful harmony arrangements. Greil Marcus, cultural critic, states that doo-wop:

"was the first form of rock & roll to take shape, to define itself as something people recognized as new, different, strange, theirs".[31]

Italians became the trendsetters for European ethnic groups along the acappella corridor. This may have been a result of their cultural love for music and their willingness to think outside the box. They and many other ethnic groups believed that they could contribute their own version of R&B group singing, and sing just like their brothers of another shade. This is the narrative that some within the Italian community espouse. Whether this story is true or not, it is well worth pondering. The Irish, on the other hand, would tend to differ and claim that they were the ones who introduced vocal group harmonization to non-African Americans, and the ethnic list can go on. Does it really matter? What matters is that these

---

[31] The Dustbin of History pg. 226 Harvard University Press ©1997 Greil Marcus

ethnic groups on the Eastern Seaboard saw how beautiful rhythm and blues group singing is and they took what they heard on the radio and made it their own. Both ethnic groups were known historically for their soaring tenors of the past century, and this led, to some degree, to the stereotype of being great singers. This can be said of blacks also; non-African Americans often believe in the stereotype that all "black folks" can sing or have rhythm. The 1950s and 1960s produced an array of Italian vocal groups, like The Belmonts from the Bronx, Heartaches, Del Capris, and Duprees from Jersey City, all of whom left an impenetrable mark on music. In Newark, there was the legendary Four Seasons and the acappella group The Savoys. All these groups had tight harmonies and solid soaring tenors. In the end, some Italian groups or lead singers have continued to this day singing in the same fashion as those who went before them. Although they are no longer the trend-setters they were decades ago, they still manage to belt out tunes reminiscent of fifty years ago.

Dion & The Belmonts

The Duprees

The Savoys Today

The late Ronnie I

7

JEWISH IMPACT ON RHYTHM AND BLUES

Contrary to what some may believe, the contribution of ethnic and racial assemblage in rock 'n' roll is significant and profound. The vocal group harmony genre, and rhythm and blues in particular was never limited to only African Americans. From the very beginning of rock 'n' roll, the vocal group rhythm and blues style of singing appealed to all young people regardless of race or ethnic background. It reflected black middle-class sentimentality and values within a restricted black vernacular. Over a period of time, rock 'n' roll and the vocal group category as a whole metastasized into non-black communities. Many ethnic groups played a role in the development of rock 'n' roll and the vocal group ethos. One such group, who lived in the urban working-class communities, was the Jewish residents who lived along the acappella corridor. The Jewish contribution to vocal group singing is unique in the development of the 1950s vocal group sound, and rock 'n' roll in general. What made the Jewish involvement unique was the ability to extract and internalize the African-American experience and make "negro music" mainstream. The Jewish contribution to doo-wop lies primarily in the area of songwriting, and the overall entrepreneurial music business. Unlike their musical counterparts—Italians, and Puerto Ricans, who were primarily performers— the Jewish contribution took on the additional role of administration and presentation of the multifaceted ethnic-racial mix of a new, emerging sound. The fundamental Jewish contribution to the rhythm and blues vocal group persona lies in production, songwriting, and the development of the vocal harmony group scene. Cahill writes:

"Without the Jews, we would see the world through different eyes, hear with different ears, even feel with different feelings".[32]

Yet when one takes a cursory view of record labels during the beginning and the development of rock 'n' roll, particularly the vocal group harmony landscape, it can be easily seen that the majority of acts, record labels, and songs written during the period (1945–1965) had a Jewish influence of some kind. The most recognizable groups and labels came from the three major epicenters that produced the vocal street-corner sound: New York, Chicago and Los Angeles. It was in these cities that the new art form became known and eventually emerged into the onomatopoeic term we use today: "doo-wop." Jewish entrepreneurs who featured black talent and promoted the new sound founded many of the major record labels during the height of the vocal group era of the 1950s. The group sound, in general, invoked a traditional cultural worldview that became the hallmark of black culture at that time.

---

[32] The Gifts of the Jews: How a Tribe of Desert Nomads Changed the Way Everyone Thinks and Feels pg. 30 1998 Thomas Cahill

T.J. Lubinsky, TJL Productions

(Courtesy WQED Radio)

Herman Lubinsky

The songs expressed by black groups reflected the cultural innocence and coming-of-age that attracted the youth of urban communities. The lyrics and musical harmony styles appealed to urban white, middle-class sentiments and, at the same time, kept their African-American musical form within the perimeter of their black community. A sizeable number of Jewish entrepreneurs had a massive impact on developing the rhythm and blues vocal group sound. Jewish entrepreneurs influenced the nascent vocal group sound of the 1950s in a dynamic way. One such person is Herman Lubinsky (Savoy Records), grandfather of T.J. Lubinsky, famous for hosting PBS "Doo-Wop" concerts. Lubinsky produced and recorded Little Anthony and the Imperials, Debutantes, Carnations, Jive Bombers, Falcons and the Robins. Lubinsky's inroad to the music business paved the way for unnoticed and unrecorded groups to seek out musical stardom via the emerging new street-corner sound. Lubinsky, like many others, loved music and relished the challenge of producing great artists. He and other people were pioneers in this new, emerging music style, which was called then "race music." They cultivated the new R&B group sound and made it palatable for cross-cultural consumption by middle-class white Americans. Lubinsky's love for African-American entertainers and his commitment to helping advance the black man musically and socially helped Savoy Records to become a major powerhouse record company. To his credit, Herman passed on his knowledge and love of music to his son, and this was passed on to T.J., who is still an ambassador to the music we love today.

The Braun family, owners of Deluxe Records, had a multitude of solid talent at their disposal. Among some of their top acts were The Federals, Otis Williams and The Charms, The Serenades, and The Quails featuring Bill Robinson. These acts were all channeled to places like the Apollo Theater in Harlem, the Olympia Arena in Detroit, and the Alan Freed show.

The team of Jerry Leiber and Mike Stoller made a multitude of hits for a host of artists. They began their career at the age of 17 and worked in the music profession for decades. As a team, they were able overcome the barriers of racism in the music industry and bring black talent to the forefront with their musical compositions. Not only did they write songs, but they also had their own record labels, Red Bird and Blue Cat, which produced many R&B recordings. Together, they were true "brothers of another shade." They worked together for sixty-one years until Leiber's death in 2011.

Another individual—and there are many more—is the late Harry Stone. Stone is one of the great record producers, like Jerry Wexler and Tom Dowd. The Bronx-born musician fell in love in what was once called, as was mentioned before, "race music." He was influential in the careers of Ray Charles, KC & the Sunshine Band and the whole R&B "Miami Sound". In actuality, he created the Miami Sound. He was instrumental in bringing acts to Miami such as Motown stars, Muscle Shoals artists, and Stax singers. His company, TK Records, was a powerhouse in South Florida. Stone put Miami on the map as a hotspot to visit for its R&B groove.[33]

---

[33] http://www.miamiherald.com/entertainment/article1979074.html

Jerry Leiber and Mike Stoller

(Courtesy George Rose/Getty Images)

Harry Stone (Courtesy of Miami Herald)

Carole King

(http://acttwomagazine.com/carole-king/)

There was also Carole King, who gave Aretha Franklin her signature cut, the soulful "You Make Me Feel Like a Natural Woman" as well as producing hits for other artists. She and her husband, Gerald Goffin, produced scores of multiple top-ten hits and made their name known in the music business as creative writers and lyricists. There is Alan Freed, The King of DJs, who cracked the color barrier by introducing black vocal groups to the public in radio, film and television, setting the stage for would-be future disc jockeys. His influence and introduction to rock 'n' roll and vocal groups provided a cultural climate whereby white youths were able to hear and experience the evolution of the new modus operandi that was beginning to shape the musical culture of young people.

Brill Building

King & Goffin

Alan Freed

Line dancing

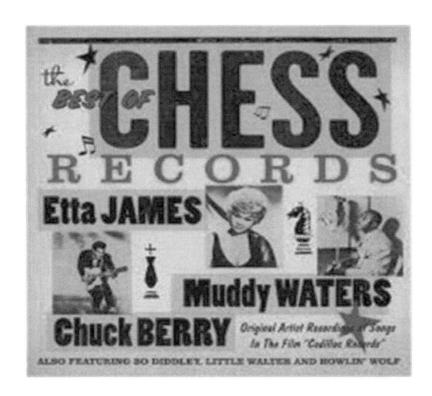

Chess Records owners – Leonard, Phil, and Marshall Chess

Chess Records, the premier record company in Chicago founded by Leonard and Phil Chess, became the quintessential record label of the 1950s. Chess produced not only groups like The Flamingos, Moonglows and others, but also top acts like Bo Diddley, Aretha Franklin, and Chuck Berry. They also included such greats as The Dells, Etta James, and The Radiants. Chess even established and produced a host of religious gospel music. In addition, this record company created a subsidiary label that was exclusively jazz: The Argo label, had a large inventory of great jazz music.

Record producer, recording engineer, and songwriter Phil Spector developed the "Wall of Sound" concept which still stands today as a monument to pop music. He produced many great acts and groups like The Ronettes, Crystals, Ike and Tina Turner, Darlene Love and Ben E. King. All of these individuals contributed to the rock 'n' roll sound and vocal group harmony in general. In the end, the Jewish contribution to rock 'n' roll and the doo-wop sound is an act of love. Their impact on music is, without a doubt, monumental and without their contribution, we would be like a ship at sea without a rudder.

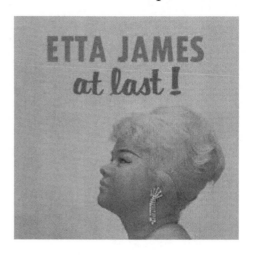

Finally, there was the legendary Jerome Solon Felder, famously known as "Doc" Pomus, a songwriter, producer and singer who was a master of creating music that touched the soul. His songs included such hits such as "Save the Last Dance for Me", "There Is Always One More Time", "Turn Me Loose I Said", and many more, totaling over 1,500 songs. Doc's love for African Americans was profound and unending. He became the first non-African American to receive the Rhythm & Blues Pioneer

Award in 1991. He was truly a soul brother in the literal sense. These individuals paved the way for undiscovered groups and artists to come to the forefront and display their talent in the public domain. The end result was that 40 percent of top artists during the mid to late 1950s were vocal groups. This is a testimony to their talent and the talent of those who promoted and recorded them. Rock 'n' roll became a financially viable undertaking that reinvigorated the industries that catered to the music, including the plastic and paper industry. Rock 'n' roll became a catalyst for employment in radio, print, and the newly emerging television industry. The embryonic middle class in America were now willing to purchase a TV set and be able to see and hear the incipient new music called rock 'n' roll, and experience vocal groups artists of a different hue in their homes. These events can be directly attributed to those early Jewish pioneers who, in their own way, broke the ethnic and color barriers and brought to light raw talent for all to experience.

Thus is the legacy of these remarkable individuals who loved the music that we call today rhythm and blues. Their inspiration, tenacity, and love paved the way for others to emulate them. However, not all was rosy among those pioneers because there was corruption and many questionable activities taking place at that time. These travesties were also true of other ethnic groups as well. The main thing is that these personalities loved the soulful music that came from heartfelt experiences that were African American. What we are left with, is the resuscitation of the vocal groups' sound that has continued for the past sixty years and continues to display itself in the style that we today call doo-wop. For this reason, we can say that the vocal group sound has made a resilient impact on music and it continues today in the form of acappella, which initially began as a vocal group sound. This is the legacy of these giants, who viewed the black vocal harmony music as exceedingly relevant to that time.

Darlene Love

The Ronettes

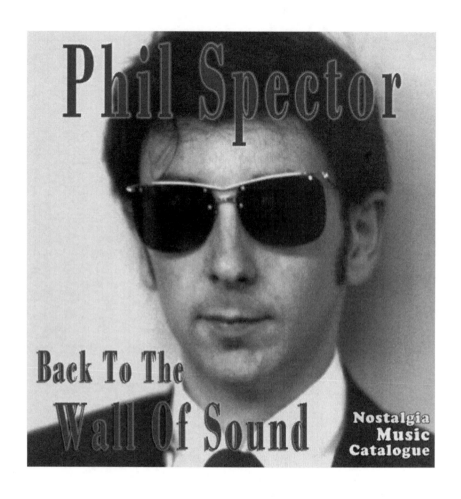

Phil Spector
Back To The
Wall Of Sound

Nostalgia
Music
Catalogue

PART THREE

MUSICAL JOURNEY

8

MIKE MILLER

The year was 1955. I was about eight years old and we were riding in my father's 1954 Packard Patrician. I was in the back seat with my brother, Ritchie. After he became the youngest first vice president of Burson -Marstellar in NY at age thirty-nine, you could only call him Richard. Every Sunday we drove up the Taconic Parkway looking at new homes. This was my father's passion. We lived in the Parkchester section of The Bronx. The radio was blaring, but I was unfulfilled. Patti Page and Tony Bennett were great, but my ears were always reaching out for the R n B sound of The Flamingos, The Harptones, The Chords, and The Moonglows.

My mother always left a radio on in my room when I was going to sleep. I would sneak out of bed and change the station to WBLS or WINS. My little ears found a sound that was pure ecstasy. Rhythm and blues, blow harmony and romantic lyrics, soon to be called Doo Wop, were what I found every night on the little Motorola transistor radio that was mine and mine alone.

I guess house hunting paid off because we moved to the very exclusive town of Armonk, NY, in a private community called Windmill Farms. I remember seeing Marilyn Maxwell sitting with Rock Hudson for lunch at the club. I remember my mother saying, "That's Rock Hudson, you know. His real name is Roy Fitzgerald." Roone Arledge of ABC sports was my neighbor. I think I even mowed his acre and a half of lawn once with my friends. For some reason, everyone in Armonk was musically inclined. There were so many fabulous guitar players everywhere. It was the late fifties and the guitar was becoming the new instrument of choice for young guys like me. I recall being four or five years old and standing on my bed with my father's tennis racquet, pretending to play the guitar and sing. Billy Bauer, the very famous Encyclopedia of Jazz guitarist and George Thorne of "I Hear a Rhapsody" fame were my teachers.

In junior high school, my mentors were Gary Dandelion, brother of the famed Armen Donelian, the jazz pianist, and Rusty Thorne - Fragos, the son of composer George Thorne. They were very accomplished musicians at a young age.

Just when I was getting comfortable in my neighborhood of musical influence, disaster set in. My parents announced that we were moving to Manhasset Hills, Long Island. Could this be true? Why was I not paying attention? How can you uproot a young guy who was going into his junior year of high school and ask him to start over in a new school? These were very impressionable years. I was the new guy at Herricks High School. I was tested immediately. What is this guy all about? Where did I fit in? There were two distinct groups. "The Sport Rats" were the "jocks" or the team guys. "The Diddley Bops" were the cool guys with the pompadours and the too tight pants. You guessed it. I was a Diddley Bop. I was a Jewish guy who hung more with the Italian guys. "I've got it!" I said all of a sudden. "Hey Pop, let's go to Sam Ash in Hempstead." Jerry and Bernice Ash, at that time only in their twenties, sold us a new Fender Jaguar, a Turner Dynamic microphone and a Fender Deluxe Reverb amplifier. "Thank you, Lord above." I found Louis Aquina and Bobby Szymanski. We became The Motions and we were high school stars. We played all the school dances in the area and all the neighborhood bars and clubs, even though we were underage at the beginning. We were making money at sixteen years old. We worked at the famous White Brick Inn and The Crazy Crickett. We talked Mario, who had a pizza restaurant on Hillside Avenue in New Hyde Park, into featuring live music on the weekends. It was great. We worked every weekend for quite a while. One week, Mario said,

"I'd like to shake it up a little." He wanted to put in a new group for some variety. We didn't mind because we had been there for six or eight weeks already. It was a group that Val Scott, a friend and very accomplished guitar player, had put together. They played oldies and surf music. Dick Dale and The Deltones had just caught on and had a few surf tunes pre Beach Boys.

They had a tall, good looking blue eyed drummer who sang and played the drums standing up. The girls loved him. This drummer was Joey Neary, whom I would sing with more than forty years later with George Galfo's Mystics. Now ain't that a kick in the head. I would love to find Val Scott.

After that, I sang and played guitar with The Dynatones. We had a steady gig at the Picture Lounge and The Camelot Inn. After that, came The Impossible Dream, The Charisma Society Orchestra, a group called Michael, (no kidding), then Grand Boulevard, and a parade of top 40 oldies groups. I even did weddings with The Joe Pastor Orchestras. I played all of the Long Island clubs. One club in particular was Saint James Infirmary in Deer Park, Long Island. It was a haven for oldies. They featured cartoons on one of the walls, the ladies room had a microphone in it and there was sawdust on the floors. The waitresses were dressed as nurses and the bartenders as doctors with stethoscopes around their necks. We backed up some of the biggest oldie groups in the country right there in Deer Park. Hold on now! During the summer of my junior year in high school, I received a phone call from Tom Giacalone who was the lead singer of The Islanders, a group that had a contract with Relic Records in Hackensack, New Jersey. They were on The Best of A cappella series. Tom was one of the most talented guys I knew. He told me that Jimmy Ponticelli was leaving the group and they wanted me to replace him. Be still my beating heart. I am now a legitimate first tenor/lead in a very well established Doo Wop Group. So there we were, Tom Giacalone, Jimmy Hanley, Howie Maher and Mike Miller, The Islanders. Wow! We hooked up with Clay Cole and opened for Johnny Maestro and The Crests at Clay Cole's World near Roosevelt Field in Long Island. It was huge and the stage was thirty feet high with a capacity of over a thousand. There were closed circuit television cameras that showed video on the opposite walls. At that time Johnny had the band, The Crests singing all the Crests hits with Joey Dee's wife, Lois. This was of course well before The Brooklyn Bridge.

Clay introduced us when we worked there. How thrilling it was for a bunch of young guys. We drove all over Long Island. Sometimes we found ourselves in Long Beach and we would get out of the car and just sing. We went to Nathans in Long Beach and would just start singing and draw a crowd. Sometimes the management liked it and sometimes they would run out and yell "Get lost McGuire Sisters!" They were foolish. They could have had a night of entertainment for a hot dog. We would go to Jones Beach and sometimes never make it to the beach while singing in the tunnel at Gate 4 because it had a great echo. We would stay there for hours and do requests. When we made it to the beach and stood on the blanket, we would draw hundreds of people who would call out tunes. We would just chime off and sing them. That is what singing groups do. They sing. We were just four guys and a pitch pipe. So good. So beautiful.

There is a song that the Islanders recorded that is unreleased. It is called "You're Such a Pretty Girl," with the flipside "Answer My Prayer." I think Stu Leibowitz had it in his jukebox at his house. We hung out there many nights. I think we wore out "The Girl I Love" by The Glowtones. We sang at a club in Queens one night, and Sandy Yaguda from The Americans was there. We were doing "Walking in the Rain" by The Ronnettes that night in our show at the club. A month or two later, Jay and The Americans recorded it. We like to fantasize that they got the idea from us.

Now signed with Gino Moretti and GMC Records, we recorded four sides in the studio. Gino used members of Maynard Fergusons Orchestra for the session. One tune was "Where the Lights Are Bright" and another was "Baby Pack On," a song written by Ray Ceroni of the Bell Notes. I remember a song written by Howie of our group called "Don't Send No Flowers," but I can't remember how it went. Wow, I would love to have those master tapes. "Baby Pack On" is now a Northern Soul Collector's Item valued at just under $200. If anyone has a clean copy or knows where Ray Ceroni is, please let me know. The Islanders were young, no-hit wonders the first time out, so with Vietnam facing us, as well as starting careers and relationships, we broke up. Looking back, we should have stayed together. It was a fabulous group with super-tight harmony and great personnel. Jay Traynor of the Americans wanted us to record his original tune, "Looking Out My Window," but it was never to be. Jay and I spoke about it on the radio recently. I still had my top forty groups and we sang a lot of Doo Wop and current tunes in the New York area. I auditioned for many Doo Wop groups over the years. I was always accepted into the group I tried out for. There were The Salutations in Brooklyn, Street Corner Society on Long Island stood out, but the timing was not good for me. I sang at weddings with The Joe Pastor Orchestras in Brooklyn. I did The Copa with my singing partner, Frankie from Mulberry Street. He was a Mafia Brat. That is a long story. Ask me about it and I will tell you the facts. I had a successful Disco group called Devoshun with Steve and Lori Adorno, Alan Korenstein, Joe Weinman, Manny Caiati and Kevin Zambrana. They were a fabulous rhythm section. We did all the big Discos in NY, got some radio play and missed having a Disco Hit not by much. I remember playing the tunes for Paco Navarro one night at Latin Sound Recording Studio. He was very distracted that night if you get my drift. He listened to our music and loved our sound. He was the top dog in NY for disco and was a DJ at WKTU, the mecca for disco in NY. The big tune was called "Dance City." People who frequented the Discos still remember it well.

Where is the Doo Wop? It was the Eighties and I was now remarried and driving to The Bronx everyday as a Dean in a tough NYC Junior High School from Danbury, Ct. My younger very successful brother was diagnosed with AIDS. It was heartbreaking. I built a small recording studio and recorded a series of tunes that I called Michael and The Dreams. I did all the parts on all the vocals and music. It was very healing for me. I called my friend Don K. Reed from CBS FM on The Doo Wop Shop and he played some of the tunes, as well as a few jingles I did for him. He said, "Michael, why don't you put a new group together?" Any time you are in spiritual or emotional pain, the music will save you. It has lifted me up more times than I can remember. Any time you can be creative, it will take you to a better place.

Harmony Street

I took what Don K. said very seriously. I wanted to sing again. I hadn't for a few years, except for a few shows at my school with the talented Kim Burgie, the nephew of Lord Burgess of "Jamaica Farewell" fame. I placed an ad in The Danbury News Times. "Lead singer looking for backup singers to sing Doo Wop. Experienced only. A long line of not so talented people marched through my den. Then I got a phone call. "My name is Dee Heavrin. I read your advertisement. I sing with two other ladies, Robin and Ellen. We call ourselves Class. Can we come over and sing for you?" Wow! I never ever thought of three ladies. I wondered what that would sound like. I said, "Sure."

They were fabulous together. They said they were going to think it over. They managed to overcome my cocky Bronx attitude and they called back and said, "Yes, we will try it." I told them that if they listened to everything I told them, we would be wonderful. They did. We were. We rehearsed about four nights a week at the beginning. We learned to breathe together, phrase together and most of all listen to each other. We listened to Manhattan Transfer religiously. Thank you, Tim Hauser for your friendship and your talent. We added bass singer Scott Poarch and with Larry Cozy Colby, who was our musical director, we became Harmony Street, which we took from a street in our home town, Danbury, Ct. I taught the girls Doo Wop as I had promised, and of course, the ladies sang it like angels, always on pitch and always ready to add their talent to the arrangement. I was in Harmony Heaven.

We were ready. I called The Danbury News Times for an article with pictures. Robin Miller, had a successful beauty salon in Bethel, NY called Hair Escape, and down the street was a restaurant named Hole in the Wall, which featured entertainment. We booked a date there and then we called Don Teig, a prominent eye doctor in Ridgefield, who just happened to have a radio show called The Doctor Doo Wop Show. He was a fabulous guy and an instant friendship was born. We were on his show a few weeks in a row. We sang live and talked about our aspirations. We even sang a jingle for him and talked about our upcoming debut. Thank you, Don, for giving us our start.

The result at Hole in the Wall was a crowd so large that we broke every fire code in Bethel, Ct. The waiters had to go outside and come in another entrance to serve the people in the back room. Harmony Street was really born that night. It grew like a spreading fire, bringing us radio interviews, clubs, dinner theaters, National Anthem opportunities and openings for big oldie shows in very large venues. Ellen Pacelli's arrangement of The National Anthem was heard in many venues. We wowed them with a twenty-five-minute show and the Anthem at Shea for The Mets during their fight for the playoffs. What a thrill that was. Rob and Laura Albanese's very first show at Queens College featured opening act Harmony Street along with The Tokens, Randy and The Rainbows, Lou Christie and a long list of top names. Bobby Jay from CBS FM was the MC that night. Ronnie Italiano, of UGHA fame, asked us to open for the UGHA 200th anniversary show at Schuetzen Park in New Jersey. I still have the handmade poster that was hanging in the lobby. It is a collector's item. I have later learned that it was handmade by Christine Vitale, who Ronnie mentored and whose show he does from The Group Harmony Alley, Sundays on 89.1/FM-WFDU.

Johnny B. (John Bunnell), from at that time WWCO in Waterbury, was a legendary DJ in Ct for many, many years. He came to hear us one night at our insistence. That night, we made a lifelong friend. We were regulars on his show. Of course, we composed a jingle for him, which he played every week. He would let me come on Sunday nights and sit in with him, taking phone calls and spinning records. I was getting DJ experience and I didn't even realize it. John made sure that we worked with every major oldie act in the business by inviting us to open up at Kennedy High School in Waterbury for every doo wop show for many years. I cannot ever thank Johnny B enough for what he did for our group. As a matter of fact, I owe him a phone call. I cannot forget my good friend, Doo Wop Don Bonomi, a friend and record collector originally from New Haven, Ct. Don was an inspiration for us. He picked songs for us, came to all of our shows and was always there for us. We were invited to his wedding to his wonderful wife, Gladys, and we maintain a friendship to this day. As a matter of fact, when he moved to Florida, he invited Ken Brady of The Casino's and me to perform at Del Webb's Stony Creek. Ken and I have a show that we do in Florida called "Doo Wop Stylings with Mike Miller and Ken Brady." It is a great 90-minute show filled with our favorite Doo Wop songs.

Along our journey, we often run into people in life who are there to help us. As luck would have it, Rick Mc Caffree and the infamous Gary Lee Schwartz of The Solid Gold Jukebox in Poughkeepsie, were two of these people. Harmony Street did their show so many times that we lost count. They were great to us. We sang live, and they played our tunes. They had me on with Kenny Vance, Jay Traynor, Mary Wilson, Darlene Love and a host of others. Gary had a portion of the show called Garyokee, where the guest group would back Gary up singing lead on a tune, and listeners would call in to guess the tune. Gary was one of the funniest guys I ever met. He once asked Johnny Maestro on the air, "Who was better looking, Alice Cooper or Tony Bennett?" When Johnny didn't want to play, Gary announced over the air, "Ladies and Gentlemen, the legendary Johnny Maestro has just been taken away for an emergency charisma bypass." Guess what folks? Johnny laughed.

Then it happened. Don't ask me how it happened. Maybe the planets were lined up correctly or the Universe smiled. I was on the White House website when I wondered, after looking at a virtual tour, whether President Bill Clinton had an email address. I found it and wrote a wonderful letter saying that we would love to come and perform The National Anthem at The White House. I clicked send and got a security screen asking some general questions. Then I clicked again. This time I got a thank you page that said, "We get thousands of emails each day. We randomly read them. Thank you for emailing the President." I forgot about it. About six weeks later, I received a letter that said, "We read your email and are very interested in Harmony Street. Please send us some promotional material." I sent pictures, a 90-minute video and a few cassette tapes. About six weeks went by, and I received a letter that said, "The President watched your video in Air Force One, on the way to China and he wants the group to come to entertain at the White House. My secretary, Danielle Westfall, will contact you." The letter was signed Capricia Penavic Marshall, secretary to the President of the United States. When Danielle called, she asked us if we could be the entertainment for The White House Christmas party in December. It all came together very nicely. It does not get any better than that. It was a forever memory. I still have the 8 x 10 portrait shot that I took with Bill that he later signed and sent back to me. From there, we had another surprise phone call. Terry Stewart, CEO of The Fox News feed that Harmony Street was going to The White House. His secretary called me and asked if we would be his guests at his New Year's Party ringing in 1999. We were now hanging with some big guns. Please pinch me.

We did many shows with Johnny Maestro and The Brooklyn Bridge. If you remember as a kid, we would open up for him on Long Island. It was great to see him again now with The Brooklyn Bridge. We even did a show together at Newtown High School, where at that time, our bass singer, Scott had children attending. It's hard to believe that a high school that we held so close to our hearts could have undergone such terrible tragedy all those years later. We think about that often.

Harmony Street mostly sold out every show they did and with the help of my good friend, Mitch Schlecter, who was like my right hand for years, we sold many cassette tapes and later, CDs and videos. He would go out into the audience with a box and was so proactive that he always came back with an empty box. They were fifteen dollars. He would offer them 2 for $10 and then $5 when there were a few left. Mitch was good and because of that, we always had a plentiful cash reserve. That meant it was time to record. We used Dennis Rivelino's studio in Westchester and eventually recorded "Harmony Street," a weepy ballad that I wrote and sang lead on, and "Christine," an up tempo original tune. It was distributed by me and Steve

Dunham on Crescent Records. We received a huge amount of air play on the oldie stations with both tunes. A bit later, we went back to the studio and recorded a version of "Lonely Way", The Skyliners' great hit and "Come Back to Me," the late great Margo Sylvia song, which Robin sang beautifully. These two tunes were, I believe, the only two songs with music on Bob Kretzchmar's Starlite Discs. We were in good company on the Starlight 2000 CD. All of these tunes continue to be heard on Doo Wop compilation CDs every year. Mickey B. used the Harmony Street tune to close out his Volume Two CD. Thank you, Mickey B, Michael. Harmony Street also appeared in a movie called "The Root of All Evil," a very B movie about trees that eat people. Ron Palillo, from Welcome Back Kotter, starred in that movie, and Scott Poarch had a role as the woodsman. Ron has since passed away in Florida.

The Ladies of Harmony Street, as I used to call them, were very unique. They had their own mystique on stage. Dee once said, "We have three times of the month in this group, and we take it all out on him." All three immediately pointed to me. I remember the time Robin sewed Randy Sufuto's button on his jacket moments before Randy and The Rainbows were called on stage. The ladies were many things to many people. Ellen Pacelli, the high soprano in the group and a super musical arranger, was also a great cook. She loved to bake, especially when we were doing one of our many shows with The Brooklyn Bridge. She loved Johnny and Grace Mastrangelo and had a very close relationship with both. One night, she made a whiskey cake and a cheesecake. When we got off the stage from doing an hour and fifteen-minute show, the cheesecake was gone. Johnny, Freddie and Les had frosting in the corners of their mouths. Johnny said, "I hope you don't mind, we ate the cheesecake". We laughed and Ellen assured them it was made for The Bridge. I reminded John that too much dairy before you sing is not beneficial to good vocals. John gave his standard answer. "It coats the throat." You can guess the rest. He was fighting to get the words out on the first tune. It got worse before it got better. Johnny was not happy till the middle of the show. He did say in the middle of that show however, "I heard Harmony Street sing "Juanita" and I realized we've been singing it wrong all these years." I loved that man and spoke to him the day before he passed away.

As a Dean in the Bronx, I had junior high school kids of all sizes, shapes and backgrounds. Two of these kids were Jimmy and Paul Keyes. They sometimes created situations that required me to call their father to my office to talk. He was of course Jimmy Keyes, the writer of "Sh Boom" and original founding member of The Chords. We became very good friends. He came to career day and dazzled a full auditorium with stories about the old days. I called Don K. Reed and got The Chords a shot on The Doo Wopp Shop. Don said that in all those years, he had never had The Chords on his radio show. Jimmy died without realizing the abundance of royalties that he and so many of the early performers deserved.

The Doo Wopp Shop

No matter how many hits, no matter how many street corners, unless you were heard on The Don K. Reed Doo Wopp Shop on CBS FM in New York, you were missing that ornament on the highest branch of The Doo Wop Tree. Don, after he played your favorite Doo Wop tune or request and the collectors' rarely heard song, turned down the lights in the studio, sent the engineer home, inched closer to the microphone, played a cut of your music and said something like, "That was Harmony Street. They will be our guests tonight on The Doo Wopp Shop." Hearts would beat very fast at the concept that thousands upon thousands of Doo Wop fans would lean into their radios on Sunday night at 11 PM EST to hear the story of your group, hear your jingle if you brought one and hear the best of your repertoire. Don played our "Rama Lama Don K. Reed" jingle on a regular basis and has told me that it was one of best on a short list that included the top names in the business. We were there many times. I would ask Don about the microphone all the way to the right that had lipstick on it. He told us that the lipstick belonged to Deborah Wetzel who did the traffic and news on CBS FM. I am happy to call Don my good friend to this day, and I applaud him for spending his entire career playing the music of our genre and supporting all of the groups who sang it. Thank you, sincerely, Don K. Reed. Don has reestablished The Doo Wopp Shop on Sunday nights at 7 PM EST on The Belmonts Internet Radio.

In the midst of a long list of concert bookings, radio interviews, a mailing list of thousands, and recognition most everywhere in northern New York and New England, I was going through a crisis. My very successful brother had succumbed to his illness. He passed away in Florida; my mother was dying from her Hepatitis C that she contracted from a transfusion during surgery and my father had Parkinson's disease and was very close to the end. I was going through a divorce, and I was really burning out at my profession as a Dean in a tough NYC junior high school.

I was flying regularly to Boca Raton, where all three of my family members lived. I decided I needed a big change. I retired from my job in The Bronx, and as sad as it was on that day, I left Harmony Street and made the decision to move to Florida. I suggested Lenny Seiter, a talented guy whom I knew at a young age, to be my replacement. Lenny fit in beautifully and the group is going strong as "In Harmony" still based in Danbury Ct.

After giving three eulogies in a very short period of time in Florida, I was emotionally and spiritually spent. I now lived in Boca Raton. Frank Iovino of The Five Boroughs called me and asked if I would sing with them, and I told him I did not have the emotional strength. I spoke to Frank Mancuso, now of The Legends of Doo Wop in Florida and formerly of The Imaginations. I knew Frank when he had a group on Long Island called Rubber Band that he sang with when the Imaginations were not working. I told him I missed singing but did not have the energy. I got a call from George Galfo of The Mystics. He was reforming a Mystic group in South Florida to be called George Galfo's Mystics. We had the necessary questions and answers, and I decided that once again, I need to sing. It was me, Shelly Brill, and Lenny Cintron of Vito and The Salutations fame. Lenny was later replaced by my old childhood friend, Joey Neary, who by then had been the high tenor on two of Dion's CDs, Nu Masters and Deja Nu. Joe was the tenor on Shu Bop, which was one of Dion's big later hits. I was now traveling, singing, writing and arranging Doo Wop.

I wrote a tune called "Husha bye Again," which I dedicated to tying the old with the new. This tune is out on Collectables Records on a CD of the same name. I had a great time on stage with George Galfo's Mystics. Many good times and memories. I produced a few CDs for them and we did some very big shows. Here I was, nearing sixty, running around singing and staying up late, coming home to a lonely Boca Raton country club. When the door latch clicked, I knew in my heart I was alone with just my own thoughts. I needed to be in love again. Enter Paulette. She showed me how to live better and how to love better. We married, I left the singing group and we settled in to make a new life. Of course, I built a new recording studio and continued to write and produce. I wrote a few new songs that have had radio play. One, called "No Ordinary Love Affair," was dedicated to Paulette. "Bouncing a Kiss Off the Moon" is a doo wop ballad from Don Riggio's Seven-Inch Vinyl: A Rock and Roll Novel, a novel which is the first part of a trilogy about a fictional group from our genre called The Du - Kanes. It follows their rise, fall and then resurrection during the late fifties, sixties and seventies. I told Don that the tune should come alive, seeing as it was their first big hit. He dared me to write it, which I did. I recorded it as the Du -Kanes doing all the music and vocals with the help of Les Levine of The Del Vikings singing the bass parts. We also did a cover of "That's the Way It Goes, "Raoul Cita's smash hit that he wrote for The Harptones. Both tunes can be downloaded on I Tunes and Amazon.

The Harmony Street Show with Mike Miller ™

As is often the case at Starbucks, people go there for first dates, to relax with friends, to do their corporate writing out of the office, to work on their computer or to just plain enjoy a venti caramel macchiato. I was leaving Starbucks in Wellington with my coffee when I heard some people at a table talking about a concert. I turned and said "What concert, blah, blah blah?" The guy turns around and says, "Who are you?" It turned out to be Peter Wein from Peter's Living Room, a popular radio show in South Florida. I told them my history in the music and Peter immediately asked, "How would you like to do a radio show?" I called some of my big name friends for advice and got the green light from everyone I called. The Harmony Street Show was born. Peter Wein was the person responsible for starting me in radio. Thank you very much, Peter. For the first year and a half, I did the show with Paulette, who is very knowledgeable about the genre. When I met her, she had a 1957 Seeburg Jukebox in the family room fully loaded with vintage doo wop. I eventually moved to Boston Internet Radio, which is now my home station. Joe Fiske and Brian West who run the station have welcomed me with open arms and have given me a great home for my show. I play a collection of main stream and obscure doo wop and rhythm and blues on the show, as well as very in depth interviews with the people who I have been on stage with over the years. I did Earl Carrolls' very last interview, as well as Clay Cole's last interview, along with Carl Gardner's very last interview, with the help of his lovely wife, Veta Gardner. It was a thrill to have Johnny Mathis on my show as well as Lloyd Price, Mary Wilson and Little Anthony, Shirley Reeves of the Shirelles and Eugene Pitt of the Jive Five. My show goes out to many other feeds such as Belmonts Radio network, owned by Warren Gradus of The Belmonts, where Don K. Reed has also found a new home. I did a show with Barry Newman and JT Carter of the Crests, Jay and The Americans, The Tymes and The Crystals not long ago. Clay Cole was the Master of Ceremonies. It made my eyes tear up to hear Clay introduce me 43 years after he introduced me the first time back on Long Island when I was a young guy. Clay's brother, Richard told me that Clay was writing a Christmas card to Paulette and myself when he got up from his desk, walked into the hallway and drew his last breath. I was honored to have him as a friend. I'm still producing shows when I have the chance. Most recently, Barry Newman and I had The Del Satins, The Brooklyn Bridge and JT Carter of The Crests at a great show in Boca Raton, Florida. I was very good friends with Earl "Speedo" Carroll and spoke to him often in the nursing home during his last days. Princess, his daughter in law, told me they used a picture that I took of Earl at his funeral. What a gentleman he was. He was a true legend. RIP Earl. My radio show is done once a week. It airs every Sunday night for the United States audience and early in the morning for the European audience. We have many thousands of listeners all over the world. When you host a radio interview show, you learn things from your guests that most people never get to hear.

Most of these facts are very interesting to our listeners who want to know more about the people whom they idolize. Are you aware that:

Larry Figueredo sat right behind Earnes Evans in elementary school in Philadelphia. When translated that means that Larry Chance sat behind Chubby Checker in elementary school. This makes alphabetical sense.

Lenny Welch once drove a taxi in NYC when he wasn't singing and he also had a recurring role on General Hospital. His longtime friend, Mel Carter had several television roles including appearances on Marcus Welby.

Who knew that Don K. Reed's mentor was the legendary Hal Jackson of WWRL Radio who had taken the time to speak to

Don during a class trip to a NY radio station when he was a youngster. Don has a picture of Hal, myself and Don taken at Rye Playland. I gave it to Don as a gift.

When Jay and The Americans were turned away by Leiber and Stoller after their audition, it was Kenny Vance's mother who told them to go right back up there and tell them "they made a big mistake and they should sign you right away." It worked.

John Madara, who wrote "Rock and Roll is Here to Stay" and "At the Hop," was Joey Heathertons first true love. Terry Stewart, the CEO of The Rock and Roll Hall of Fame, was originally The CEO of Marvel Comics who produced Spiderman and gave us all of those superheroes.

Tim Hauser of Manhattan Transfer was a baseball player.

Dodie Stevens, who sang "Tan Shoes and Pink Shoe Laces," sang with Sergio Mendes and Brazil 77 for many years.

Lloyd Price wrote all of his hits, owned all of the publishing and all of the record labels that he recorded. This means he owned all the means of production including the distribution. He owed nothing to anyone. He did not have to chase anyone for royalties as did so many of the greats from years gone by.

Johnny Mathis, after listening to his newly recorded offering of "When Sunny Gets Blue" on the radio, admitted that he sang it wrong. I asked Little Anthony once if the smoke at The Brooklyn Fox Theater bothered him on stage because in those days, at the Murray The K shows, they smoked in the theater. He told me it didn't because he would put the cigarette out on his heel just before he walked out on stage. Joey Dee told me when I was just 17 years old that I should always get paid before

I put one foot on the stage. I told him that that would work for him because he was Joey Dee, and I was just Mike Miller.

Living in south Florida is wonderful. It is also a mecca for singers who sang our music. So many of them have moved here to appreciate not only the Baby Boomers who are their fans, but also the fabulous warm weather. Dion, Jimmy Gallagher of The Passions, Terry and Theresa Johnson of The Flamingos, Gene Chandler, Joe LoCicero of The Chimes, Frank Mancuso of The Imaginations, Tony Passalaqua of The Fascinators, Frank Iovino of The Bob Knight Four and The Five Boroughs, Ken Brady of The Casinos, Connie Francis, Herman Santiago of The Teenagers, Barry Newman, Johnny Contino, Vito Balsamo of The Salutations, Joe Karp, Phil Cracolici, George Galfo and Joe Neary of The Mystics, Eddie Pardocchi of The Five Discs, and Lola and Tom Foy of The Impalas and The Saints, are just some of the names who have found a home in Florida. This would make a fabulous super group.

Every week I learn something new about the music that I love. I marvel at the audiences that still come to hear the tunes of the Fifties and Sixties. You may have bank presidents sitting next to the person who does their landscaping. You may have the waiter who served your last meal at your favorite restaurant or the guy who does the used car commercial at the dealership down the road all sitting shoulder to shoulder with one common goal. They all yearn to be magically beckoned back to their youth remembering the songs and the events that brought them forward through their journey in life. Each one remembers it differently, but the songs are the same and they want to hear them exactly the way they remember them. I have sung every genre of music from Rock to Disco and back.

There is no music so pure or so spiritual as a few guys standing on the corner with only their voices making tight vocal harmony with each other. It is hard to explain the ability to just chime off and sing a song naturally without pause. I have heard many talented singers who were unable to capture a true Doo Wop quality. I offer you this. I am thrilled to be a small pebble on a big beautiful and wonderful beach that encompasses our genre of music filled with sand castles and beautiful waves and shells. When I look out over the horizon and see the many greats that have paved the way and have gone before us, I imagine those fabulous harmonies that inspired us to emulate them and to be creative in our own right. There is no music that fills me up more than the street corner sound. You may call it Rhythm and Blues or just call it Doo Wop. It doesn't matter; it will live forever.

White House East Room Christmas 1998

9

JERRY LAWSON

Jerry Lawson is the former lead singer, arranger, producer, and Godfather of contemporary acappella. Lawson's voice, as lead singer of The Persuasions is a national vocal treasure on par with Sam Cooke, Curtis Mayfield, Otis Redding, Jerry Butler and Nat King Cole. Through the decades, Lawson's fans and collaborators have included Frank Zappa, Stevie Wonder, Ray Charles, Paul Simon, Joni Mitchell, Rod Stewart, the Grateful Dead, and Liza Minnelli. Jerry was born in Ft Lauderdale, Florida, moving to Brooklyn N.Y. as a young man, where he and the other four original Persuasions began their 40-year career together. After decades of carrying the acappella torch largely alone, Lawson's departure in 2003 ended The Persuasions' 40-year run. But launching a solo career, thinking he was "done with acappella forever" didn't quite work out. Lawson could not resist pairing up with the veteran San Francisco vocal group, Talk of the Town. Together, they recorded his magnum opus a cappella album, "Jerry Lawson & Talk of The Town", in 2007---a triumph of 20 of Lawson-arranged tunes from gospel to ballads to rock to blues.

Between this and doing gigs with R&B and jazz groups in his adopted city of Phoenix, Arizona, he also began a career working with developmentally disabled adults. In 2015, at age 71 his baritone pipes honed and honeyed, Lawson released his debut solo album, "Just a Mortal Man," produced by Nashville's Grammy-nominated Eric Brace. The album title was almost his epitaph. (While in the hospital for a knee replacement, he developed a lethal infection that nearly took his life. Somehow, he battled back, with body, spirit, and trademark voice intact.) With a host of some of Nashville's finest musicians backing him, Lawson created an elegant, polished work that is a tour-de-force for his one-of-a-kind voice, covering everything from gentle country to rock 'n' roll. He co-wrote one of the songs, "Woman in White," with Grateful Dead lyricist Robert Hunter, and finally got to do "Just a Mortal Man," with a band. As of this printing, the album is getting nothing---nothing---but breathless, panting endorsements. "Perhaps the greatest vocalist of his generation you haven't heard of." ---Music News. In 2015, this living legend is still at the top of his game---touring behind his first-ever solo album. "Jerry Lawson is a great stylist with an infallible instinct for the essence of every song he sings. With the Persuasions Jerry Lawson made many great recordings, but Just a Mortal Man is his finest hour, a master class in basic human emotions in all their complexity and inscrutability". David McGee-Deep Roots Magazine

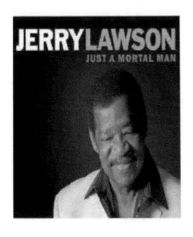 

The Persuasions - a short history

In 1969, Frank Zappa heard The Persuasions singing live over the phone in a New Jersey record shop, picked his jaw up off the ground and promptly flew the group to Los Angeles to record their first album, "Acappella". Thus began a 22-album recording career that focused on R&B, soul, and pop but also included full album tributes to Frank Zappa, The Grateful Dead and The Beatles, and even an acclaimed children's album. Through it all, The Persuasions' sound was defined by Lawson's sweet and smoky baritone, his effortlessly organic vocal arrangements, and his electrifying stage charisma. The group has been universally lauded as the "Kings of Acappella", with modern groups such as Take 6, Rockapella, The Nylons, 14 Karat Soul, and Boyz II Men citing them as a major influence.

Julie and Jerry Lawson

10

JOE CALAMITO

The Heartaches began back at Holy Rosary Grammar school in Downtown Jersey City, New Jersey sometime around 1961. Back then, they were called the Vydells. Joe Calamito started the original group after watching American Bandstand. He decided he wanted to sing bass in a doo-wop group. Having no idea how to begin, Joe Calamito talked a few friends in trying to sing at a grammar school class night program. He recruited the help of one of the star football players on the Holy Rosary football team, Tommy D'Alessandro. Joe Calamito and Tommy D'Alessandro's friendship has spanned more than 40 years and lead them on a vocal journey that lasted 30 years where they performed with some of the best vocal artists on the American doo-wop and top 40 scenes. After a disastrous performance at the grammar school class night. Joe Calamito and Tommy D'Alessandro realized that what they needed was better singers and more rehearsal-lots more. After trying -retrying and trying different singers, they found the perfect vocal blend in what became known as Joanne and the Heartaches, and then finally just the Heartaches.

The original Heartaches Joe Calamito bass- baritone, Tommy D'Alessandro,2nd tenor, Charlie Romano tenor, Bobby Taglarini tenor and, lead singer Joanne Lucas spent two years listening to the radio and practicing songs they heard and liked and then attempted to put them into acappella renditions. The Original Heartaches worked hard to achieve their own style and blend of harmony and at that time became known as "Blue Eyed Soul group." In 1964, they entered a state talent contest and were awarded third place. This lead to various performances in and around New Jersey. In 1965, they signed a recording contract with Stan Krause's Catamount record label. In the summer of 1966 "I' m So Young" b/w A Lover's Call an original song by Calamito was released. They appeared at many more shows especially the legendary State Theater in Hackensack NJ along with The Royal Counts, The Concepts and the Persuasions and many of the early acapella doo-wop groups, the Zircons, the Delstars etc. The Heartaches became known for their female lead-four man back up harmony. In 1967, the lead vocal shifted from Joanne Lucas to Gerry O'Neil.

In 1968, Joanne Bevaqua and Russell Capo were added. They were now called the "Heartaches" They performed in and around the metropolitan area until 1969 when the group stopped performing after Calamito entered the United Sates Army. In 1971, an attempt to regroup took place but only for a few months. However, Joe Calamito and Tommy D'Alessandro continued to sing with Russ Capo and became known as the "Neighborhood Wish" Performing at Ronnie I's UGHA. There they performed with an acoustic guitar played by Calamito and singing originals by Crosby Still and Nash and others from 1970s. Fortunately, this was short lived and the group broke up.

The story would end here, but Calamito and D'Alessandro were persistent to continue on and in 1981 along with Raul Vicente and Phil Granito (he now sings with the Dupree's) united for what would be the most popular Heartaches to date. This four-man vocal powerhouse performed with many of the rock and roll greats. They won a contest sponsored by Richard Nader in 1983 and performed at Madison Square Garden. They appeared on the Americana Circuit and countless shows at Club Bene and Hoboken's Mile Square City nightclub. Appearing with most of the legends of early doo-wop era. They sang backup on two children's Album's, sang backup on a disco hit in the UK for a performer named Choppers. The Heartaches sang the voice over on a Sassoon Jeans Commercial. Their group performed on the Joe Franklin show, The Don K Reed radio show and eventually signed a production contract with Lou and Dave productions, which would lead to a one-year contract with RCA records in1985. Unfortunately, in 1985 Phil Granito left the act to peruse other interests. As a result, the sound was not the same. The remaining members Joe Calamito, Tommy

D'Alessandro, and Raul Vicente added a four-man band behind them and performed for 5 more years as the musical version of the Heartaches. In 1990, the group disbanded.

All the original members of the Heartaches have remained friends over the years, a bond that was established in the echo of a hallway, the bright lights of a school auditorium stage. The Heartaches like many of their counterparts who came to sing never achieved the "hit" record. Nonetheless, they do hold a place as one of the early pioneers of A cappella and their efforts, along with all the groups who performed in the early years.

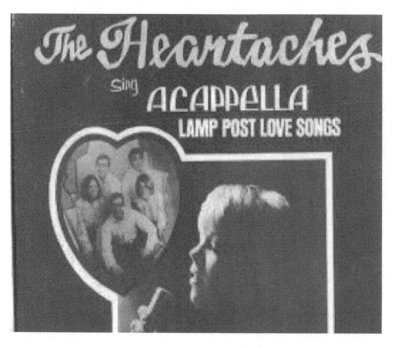

11

EDWIN F. RIVERA

I am one of five children and come from a musical family. Both my Mom and Dad were very active in their church choirs. My older sister graduated from college on six scholarships for music, she was a contralto-soprano. The running joke in our family was that even our family dog barked well and in tune. I have been singing ever since I can remember. I was in a school and church choir from the age of five but did not get into vocal group singing until the age of thirteen. We grew up in Jersey City, New Jersey, during the gang era, late 1950s thru the 60s. So to survive, one had to belong to a gang for protection. Jersey City had different ethnic areas, the Italian section, Hispanic, Black, Irish, and Jewish section, etc. I can remember my first Doo wop influences, The Flamingos, Tony Williams and The Platters, Lee Andrew and the Hearts, The Passions, The Five

Satins, Willy Winfield and The Harptones, Four Seasons, Del-Vikings, Johnny Maestro and the Crest, Vito and the Salutations and many more, which I can't remember at this writing. I remember memorizing all the lyrics of songs at that time. I could sing alto tenor and had a great falsetto, but my real passion became making harmony in the background.

In High School, I joined the vocal choir and eventually became the president of the choir in my senior year. I started as a first tenor but got into the habit of always trying to sing bass and over four years, I turned myself into a baritone vocally. Within our gang, there were three other guys that also liked to sing, Juan Perez nickname Puly, who sang first tenor, Abe Santiago nickname Buba, who sang second tenor and Amed Valentine who sang lead and myself nickname Reb singing baritone. We originally called ourselves The Five Latins for a short time even though there were four of us. In due course, we called ourselves "The Concepts". Like the typical stereotype doo-wop group of the time, we would hang out in our turf usually under a street lamp, hallway, or somewhere where we could get some type of acoustic sound. Listening to music and trying to copy and reproduce the same harmonies we heard on the radio or on records was our goal. We always had other guys that wanted to get in on the act, but in the end it was the four of us that would work out the harmonies and sing to a crowd and most importantly, tried to impress the ladies from our crowd. We would also enter any and all talent shows and contests that were available to gain recognition for the group.

We all attended the same high school, James J. Ferris in Jersey City. Jersey City has four public high schools, Dickenson, Lincoln, Snyder, and Ferris. Ethnically, Dickenson was considered predominantly white, Snyder and Lincoln, largely black and Ferris was the most integrated of the four, having Hispanics, Blacks and White students. As a result, we had four vocal groups, an all-girl group made up of Hispanic and Black singers, an all-white mainly Italian, a Puerto Rican group (that was us), and an all-Black group. Whenever we had auditorium assembly, the principal Dr. Finn our school principle would allow one of the four groups to sing and once a year they would let us have a battle of the groups, musically.

It was during our high school years that we met Stan Krause, who owned a record shop, which still survives to this day in Journal Square. Stan had a record label called Catamount Records and we recorded a forty-five single. The song we recorded was called "The Vow" and on the other side, a song in Spanish "Yo me Pregunto" translated- I ask myself. We all graduated from high school and went our separate ways. Abe, Puly, and Amed went into the Air force, I joined the Navy.

I finished my military duty as a medical corpsman and went to lab tech school. I got married, had two great boys, and worked as a lab tech until the advent of emergency medical technicians, at which point I became an ambulance Emergency Medical Technician or EMT. This I did until the start of the Physician Assistant program, at which point I applied and was accepted to the Harlem Hospital Center Physician Assistant Program. I graduated in 1977 and began working as a PA in Manhattan. During this period, I was at a family social function and music was playing. Several of us, were singing along to the music, when someone stopped the tape and noticed that we were singing in harmony. This was the beginning of "HARBORSIDE", a seven-man band, four vocalists and three instrumentalists. We have played together, the same seven guys for thirty years. We recorded one LP, one CD and one single 45. Eventually, Harborside was doing less and less singing at that time. Otis Harper, our second tenor was also singing with his old group Memory. His group was not doing much singing either, and eventually he and his friends formed a new group called "*Desire*". Otis's group needed a baritone, so Otis called me, I sat in on a rehearsal with these guys and now seven years later, we're still singing and getting better at it. We have recorded one CD and are working on our second one.

We have opened up for Jay Leno at the Sands Casino in Bethlehem Pennsylvania in August 2012. We have also played at the Sands Casino in Bethlehem, Pa. We are scheduled to play there three times this year 2015, February, June, and October. We have also played for PNC-Bank at Caesar's Palace in Atlantic City. We are very popular in the New Jersey, New York, Connecticut, and Pennsylvania area. We still rehearse once a week and gig approximately twice a month. Doo Wop has gotten into my blood and I have become addicted to it. Balanced, well-blended harmony is my high. I have taught Doo Wop clinics and have told the participants, when you can sing your part confidently then you can enjoy listening to the harmonies and this is what it's all about, as far as am concerned.

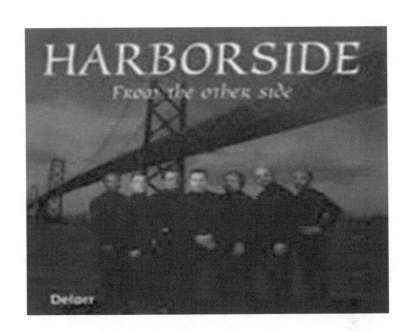

The Concepts

Desire

12

VAL SHIVELY

I thought I had it all together. I turned a hobby into a successful business, had a beautiful wife, had money, had a lot of friends, and was generally liked and respected. Even though I had all this, I wasn't happy. I was always negative. My favorite expressions were, "I never had a good day." I buried myself in my work. My work was my life. Then one day...CRASH! I lost my mind and my passion for everything (work, people, music, and food). Nothing meant anything. I was on automatic pilot for almost a year. When my wife Patty wouldn't take it anymore, she and I tried "couples counseling" as a last resort. After many sessions that weren't bringing me out of my funk, the counselor said, "Maybe it's a spiritual thing...do you go to church?" I told her no, I live the by the Golden Rule. "Do unto others..." I told her that I knew too many people who attended church and live anything but a Christian life. But...the seed was sown, and I decided to explore it. Patty and I first went to traditional churches, then a non-denominational one that I liked better. The fourth Sunday I decided to try the storefront church across the street from my store. It was unlike any church I ever attended—no crosses, no sign of Jesus---just a room with a lot of chairs.

At the end of the service, the pastor pulled an altar call, which I answered. I prayed a sinner's prayer with a young person who assisted me. When I walked outside, the heavens opened up to me! All the negativity, sin and stuff that choked my life were lifted off. I felt completely new...free and happy! A feeling I never felt before. It was a miracle—could accepting Jesus in your life and repenting from your old like do this? WOW! A few weeks later, I was baptized. That was over 10 years ago. Since then, my life has taken a new turn. I try to put the Lord first, read the Bible, tithe, and start and end each day in prayer.

Before I received the Lord, I worshipped money and its power. I did business practices and things in my life that weren't always "the right thing". I had the filthiest mouth and like most people, I thought possessions gave you happiness. That's probably why I was everything but "happy". I'm so grateful to God for all his blessings. I'm still married to Patty (we just celebrated our 20th anniversary). I work less and try to spend more time together. I still love my work, although it's not as important as it was. God knocked it out of first place, where I had it in front of Patty, family, and friends. God works in mysterious ways. His ways aren't our ways. If my life hadn't taken the nosedive it did, I wouldn't have God, the joy, and the peace of mind that comes from serving him today. So...when things are not good in your life, maybe it's God's way of getting your attention and preparing you for a new life or journey. I'm nobody special and He did it for me, so He can do it for you too. So, if you want true happiness and joy, and a secure future (eternity in Heaven), love and serve Jesus beginning today, if you don't already. P.S. We're not promised tomorrow. Look at the 3000 people who went to work on 9-11.

13

KENNETH BANK

Growing up on the hard streets of Washington Heights I made my bones or earned my street creds by earning the respect of guys with names like Specs, Whitey, Tex, Porkie, and Joey. I looked up to these guys because they were older than me by about 2 years and when you are 14 that is a huge difference. They were street fighters and some of the baddest dudes in uptown Manhattan. When they weren't figuring out how to steal stuff from the freight cars that ran along the Hudson River, or harassing the building superintendents on the street, they were getting ready to "rumble" with other neighborhood groups over petty shit. Stickball was the game every day and going to "sets" (parties) where everyone brought their 45's and slow danced to a red light while "grinding" with the chick you had your eyes on during the week before was what we looked forward to. The songs we played were some of the most beautiful music I had ever heard. The Paragons, Jesters, Jive Five, Flamingos, Heartbeats, and Drifters all provided the musical accompaniment to our education in the seduction of the opposite sex.

But what also got my attention were the sounds that would come through my window at night from somewhere down below. Intertwined with the Latin music that always played in Spanish Harlem, guys were singing in a building lobby or under the street lights somewhere. No instruments just acappella. These full rich melodies and background harmonies went straight to my soul. I became hooked and every evening I would finish my homework and wait to listen to the sounds as if I had a radio. I learned every song and sang in my room while they sang somewhere down below. Then one day I was coming home from the gym late. I walked past the lobby of a building and the guys were inside singing. So I stopped and Whitey spotted me and waived me inside. These lobbies were all made with marble and the echo was great. The fellas were having trouble with a song so I offered to help and stepped in as a second tenor/lead and helped them with their individual parts. I started making music with the guys I looked up to and they were looking at me very differently now. My life was never the same after that. I was not looking for an echo any more, I had found it, embraced it and I ran with it.

There we were. Three Puerto Ricans making music acapella in Washington Heights and/or Harlem depending upon who you were trying to impress. I loved it! It didn't hurt that the ladies were noticing too. Frankie, Sal and I formed a small social club called the Half Angels. We became the nucleus for a singing group that rotated lead singers in and out but our background was constant and the sound was soulful and rich. The Half Angels social club became the vehicle for trips to other neighborhoods so we could go to "sets" or just sing. Of course travelling to other neighborhoods had its dangers. The fellas living there did not exactly welcome us to their turf for fear we were attracting or trying to "pull" their ladies. Well even if we promised not to some things were inevitable. Somehow, I became a lot faster on my feet, as our preference was to be social animals rather than fighters so when we could we ran, fast. But lines always blurred and we had our fair share of scrapes, bloody faces and an occasional stabbing. In the following two years my life began to change in a big way. As my hormones were beginning to rage, girls became the number one distraction, and singing was my number one passion, not school. I know that's crazy, right? Those streets were harsh. And the best way to get over in life was to get out. School was the path but an echo was my spiritual guide. The fellas I used to run with were all now heading off to the Army, which seemed like a world away but in some way mysterious to me. I found that I was envious of them. The mystique of serving your country and becoming a real man lingered with me. My uncles and brothers all served and it just seemed like perhaps that was the thing to do. But I had time, because now I needed to focus on graduating high school and looking for a college. My echo was maturing and rounding itself out all the while keeping center stage. My confidence grew in leaps and bounds as my prospects for the future were looking good.

I was in the top high school in New York, being trained to be an engineer. The Half Angels were making their own reputation. And most importantly, I found that singing in subways was becoming a religious experience. The curved tunnels covered in tile made the four or five of us sound like a twelve-man chorus. That echo became my tuning fork that would resonate inside of me. The vibrations I felt would stir nerve endings I never knew I had. Not only had I found it but my echo was now inside me.

The Five Sharks

Ken & Lorna Bank

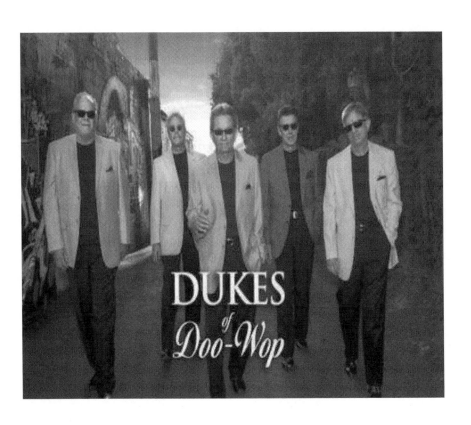

PART FOUR

PAST, PRESENT, AND FUTURE

14

NEWARK AND BOWERS AVENUE

"People have to see that there is a high degree of complexity about belonging to a gang. It's a symptom, not a problem."
Greg Boyle

In many urban communities during the 1950s and 1960s, singing and forming vocal groups was a way out of juvenile delinquency and initiation into gang activity. However, in some cases, singing groups were really an extension of street gangs. Singing groups acted as a social catalyst for their members. Vocal groups served as "fronts" in some cases; gang members would enlist vocal groups to attend their social club functions with the hopes of drawing young people. It worked well for both parties. Vocal groups would sing in their gang social setting and draw a host of teens to hear the group sing. In many cases, gangs would designate a building, connected parish facility, or storefront to hang out. Various hangouts became the focus for music, dancing, playing pool, Ping-Pong, and entertaining. A case in point is the street gangs Chancellors and Park Boys of Jersey City during the 1960s. The Chancellors, a Puerto Rican street gang, and the Park Boys, an Irish gang, epitomized the ethnic differences that existed between these two groups. Members of both gangs had one or more individuals who were "loosely associated" with a vocal group of some kind. Gangs offered something that teenagers were looking for; they were able to give something tangible to their potential recruits. Becoming a participant meant that gang members were now family.

The Concepts

The Del Capris

The Chancellors of Jersey City, New Jersey

Street gangs created a spirit of camaraderie, respect, and prestige, the very things all young people were looking for, especially guys. The squaring off of a neighborhood borderline provided a backdrop of tension that existed between rivals.

What ended the friction was the ability of the singing groups to enter their opponents' neighborhoods, not as gang members but as singers. Vocal groups, in reality, were ambassadors to their gang and their cultural community. Keep in mind that many singers were "loosely connected" to their ethnic gangs. They would not be considered, by any stretch of the imagination, hoodlums. They both were associated with gangs because of their ethnic and cultural background. Cultural and ethnic insularity among ethnic groups of all kinds was prevalent during this time period.

As was mentioned before, the ending of strife between these two gangs in Jersey City and within the Hudson River enclave was music. It was their love of rhythm and blues that glued them together, not as enemies, but as friends and competitors. The transformation of attitudes between these two ethnic groups and others was the bridge that brought them together on an equal footing. New York City was the center for the transformation of entire neighborhoods. It began in the 1950s and came across to the other side of the Hudson River.

By way of example, Puerto Ricans became the new people on the block searching for the American Dream. In many cases, the transformation of a neighborhood or "white flight" took place within a decade or two. There was no such term as gentrification; it was a community changing and replacing current residents for Puerto Ricans.

West Side Story best depicts how it was during this time. Perhaps the best social commentary was the story written by David Wilkerson in his book, The Cross and the Switchblade, which has sold millions of copies and has been translated into various languages. It became a film in the early 1970s. The Mau

Maus were a Puerto Rican street gang from New York City that made headlines for a crime they committed. The result was that their gang broke up, and their leader Nicky Cruz experienced forgiveness of sins and a new beginning by turning his life over to Jesus Christ. David Wilkerson was responsible for proclaiming the love of God to Nicky and his gang. Wilkerson wrote The Cross and the Switchblade based on the experience he had with teenagers and it became an international bestseller. Pat Boone and Erik Estrada performed in a film that was based on the book. Wilkerson started Teen Challenge, and it still exists today.

The bottom line to this is that many urban singing groups were formed out of loosely connected street gangs. Some gangs were Irish, Jewish, or black, yet in all this, the breaking down of stereotypes emerged, and teenagers looked at each other in a more tolerant and accepting way. Among other factors, it was street corner singing that contributed and paved the way for helping create an atmosphere of peace, tranquility, and reconciliation. This took place in urban America, and more specifically, along the acappella corridor. Also the war in Vietnam drafted urban youths out of poor and working class communities and into a new world of discipline and service for their country.

With the breaking down of stereotypes among various ethnic and racial groups, music became a springboard into the introduction of different musical fusions. Latin Soul in Spanish Harlem, for example, became the new musical genre in New York City during the 1960s. It was a fusion of soul, brass, and percussions with a dash of vocal group singing in both Spanish and English. Joe Bataan with his album Riot exemplifies the fusion of this new sound during the 1960s. Very different from what took place during the 1950s when various ethnic groups disliked each other. Tolerance and acceptance of each other culturally and ethnically was brought about by music. Music became the bridge to communities, and the radio helped propel that music to neighborhoods. The culture of America was changing, and it contributed to the attitude that peace is better than conflict. It is within this framework that various musical genres flourished.

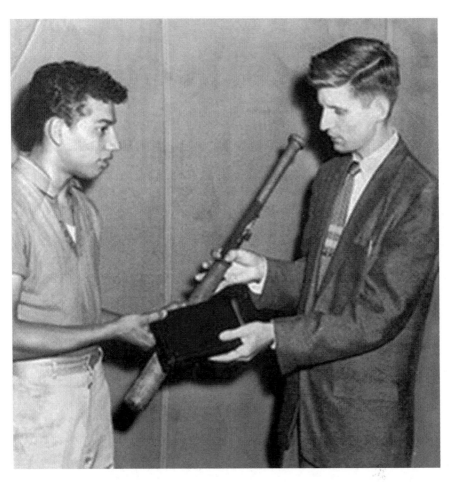

Nicky Cruz and David Wilkerson

Lastly, former gang members who were once involved in delinquency took advantage of the peace and tranquility that was going on and became entrepreneurial business persons. Some started businesses, some worked for the federal government, and some went to college, military, and some became leaders in the community as politicians. Others served in the local city and became law enforcement officers. Most of all, countless individuals looked outside of their own small, ethnic world and explored things beyond their own cultural sphere. This all took place as a result of events that were going on and the opportunity that was available for those who worked hard and put their time into being a success. Scores of young adults became successful through hard work and not through special treatment because of their ethnic or racial background. They all epitomized that hard work brings success and that anyone can achieve their dream regardless of obstacles. Those who were former street gang members are now enjoying the fruit of their labor as retirees and enjoying their grandchildren. Some members are still singing, others are consultants, and some are world travelers. Music became the bridge that ended the strife and conflict among so many ethnic groups along the acappella corridor.

15

THE HEALING POWER OF GOOD MUSIC

When Marvin Gaye produced the hit song "Sexual Healing" in 1982, young people were thrilled that perhaps sex can heal the soul and mend relationships. In 2011, it was uploaded without musical instrumentation as an acappella cut on YouTube. When a person listens to the lyrics of Gaye's hit song, it is full of narcissistic lines that center on him alone. The lyrics of his song indicate self-absorption of himself.

"Ooh, now let's get down tonight, Baby. I'm hot just like an oven. I need some lovin'. And baby, I can't hold it much longer. It's getting stronger and stronger. And when I get that feeling I want Sexual Healing, Sexual Healing. Oh baby, makes me feel so fine, helps to relieve my mind. Sexual Healing, baby, is good for me. Sexual Healing is something that's good for me. Whenever blue tear drops are falling, and my emotional stability is leaving me, there is something I can do. I can get on the telephone and call you up, baby, and Honey, I know you'll be there to relieve me. The love you give to me will free me. If you don't know the things you're dealing, I can tell you, darling, that it's Sexual Healing. Get up, get up, get up, get up, let's make love tonight. Wake up, wake up, wake up, wake up, 'cuz you do it right, Baby. I got sick this morning. A sea was storming inside of me, Baby. I think I'm capsizing. The waves are rising and rising. And when I get that feeling, I want Sexual Healing. Sexual Healing is good for me. Makes me feel so fine. It's such a rush, helps to relieve the mind, and it's good for us. Sexual Healing, baby, is good for me. Sexual Healing is something that's good for me. And it's good for me, and it's

good to me, my baby, ohhh. Come take control. Just grab a hold of my body and mind. Soon we'll be making it, Honey. Oh, we're feeling fine. You're my medicine. Open up and let me in. Darling, you're so great. I can't wait for you to operate. I can't wait for you to operate. When I get this feeling, I need Sexual Healing".[34]

Good music does heal. Good music lifts the soul and sex does heal the soul or spirit within the confines of marriage. As in the case of Marvin's song, it is self-centered. Gaye may very well have been suffering from NPD or narcissistic personality disorder. In the 1960s, sex was the theme for bringing people together. The slogan "Make love, not war" meant having sex in order to bring peace, dialogue, and healing. It opened the floodgates of promiscuity and the rejection of moral absolutes. It resulted in young people contracting sexually transmitted diseases, unwanted pregnancies, dropping out of school, shattered home life, and disillusionment with self. In 1966, Time magazine had "Is God Dead?" on its front cover. Many young people's worldview was that of contempt toward God or spirituality. Good music is not centered on the self exclusively. However, this present generation does not musically compare to the decades of the 1950s and '60s. Songs then were structured flawlessly. Music was geared at teens as a whole. Musical hits dealt with themes of love, jealousy, rejection, and teenagers coming to terms with how to deal with those issues. The tugging, heartfelt melodies of songwriters with their lyrics captured the attitude and the language of their audience's inner experiences. The accuracy of what was heard on the radio in the 1950s and 1960s resonated with teens of all social, economic,

---

[34] http://www.azlyrics.com/lyrics/marvingaye/sexualhealing.html

and racial-ethnic backgrounds. Songwriters knew the basic writing skills of how to use subtle chord manipulation and instrumental counterpoints to make their music go far.

When one explores the music in the context of that generation, we see that music was more creative lyrically than what we have today. The reason vocal group harmonization has sustained itself for decades is partly because of the beautiful lyrics that were composed and the vocal harmonies it produced. They reflect, to a small degree, naiveté and a reflection of the culture that was changing at that time.

This brings us to the concept of healing. Music has the power to soothe and heal. The whole concept of healing through music is thousands of years old. The ancient Hebrews knew the healing power of music, and this is evident in the story of David and King Saul who was beset by an evil spirit. Some of the music from the 1950s and '60s did have elements that lifted the inner person to heights of pleasure and enjoyment. The pop hit song "Oh Happy Day" that was recorded in 1969 by the Edwin Hawkins Singers reached number four on the U.S. pop charts. You do not have to be a spiritual person to fall into a groove and start singing the words of that song. For example, "So in Love" by the Tymes, Ruby and the Romantics' "Our Day Will Come", or "One Fine Day" by the Chiffons all have that quality of solid, meaningful lyrics with good background vocals and a beautiful melody. It is not just pop music, but if we go back into the classical era, we see how good music sustains itself. The classical works of Beethoven, Hayden, Bach, and others have demonstrated that classical music also soothes the spirit and brings healing. There is enough scientific and clinical evidence to prove that music is therapeutic.

Music does a number of things that affect our overall mind and body. When we listen to music, it releases certain chemicals, such as dopamine, which are essential for a healthy nervous system. Music also affects the heart rate, reduces anxiety, and combats depression. Music is the best antidote for people of all ages who need a buzz instead of a drug to help us feel good. Yet it appears that the music we hear today is lacking in the basic core elements that can inspire us to reach those emotional highs. Many of the pop songs that are on the airwaves today do not inspire, but rather encourage a base behavior that is self-centered, ugly, and full of hate. Anyone who has heard songs on the radio knows well what type of music is out there influencing young adults. The vocal group harmonization genre does lift the spirit in many ways. The vocal harmonies bring us to another sphere of musical enjoyment. The close-knit voices that blend together act like a blanket that covers our body and radiates a joyful memory of the past and present. That is why this genre is on the rise, and it appears it will not abate anytime in the near future. The increasing popularity of this art form is growing, and as it continues to grow, it is having a ripple effect thanks to good marketing skills by some vocal group enthusiasts. However, we can again thank people like Derek Sharon and Dr. Charles and Pam Horner, who are far apart in terms of vocal genre style, but are one in their love for music. Both love the human voice, yet both have a different bent on group singing. Sharon loves ensembles and collegiate acappella singing. Dr. Horner's love is contained within classic R&B vocal group singing. Both individuals are having an impact. Sharon is writing, producing, and arranging works for TV, theatre, and film. Horner is teaching and lecturing on film, public platforms, and institutions. The more our music is perpetuated to the public, the more we receive those pleasurable moments of the past.

As one studies the lyrics of songs written from the 1950s and 1960s, we can see elements of truth being sung by vocal artists. In many cases, songwriters were writing from their own experience and their own emotional, heartfelt emotions as they experienced them. What they wrote translated into pop hits that resonated with young people and adults. This is the power of truth. Truth always prevails over falsehood. Truth prevails over all things, and unfortunately, some songwriters, DJs, singers, music industry, corporate executives prefer music that only sells records. It does not matter if music promotes hate, vulgarity, or if the artist is a misogynist. The end result is that records are sold, producers make money, and the artist becomes a celebrity.

Good music should soothe or bring healing, emotionally and psychologically. Music is cross-cultural and has no borders or boundaries. Good music engages people to think and pricks our conscience to respond or not respond to what we are hearing. In music, we can respond to what we hear on an emotional level and begin to dance or sway or just ignore it. For most people, we respond to music on an emotional level. We connect and we become transfixed by what we are hearing, and we usually block out any interruptions, which is easy to do with our headphones. We become transported to a new dimension of sight and sound in our world of high-tech. Nevertheless, in many cases, after the music is over, the same nagging, unresolved issues may still be there. Our concerns, in some cases, are heavy with guilt weighing us down to the point that we want another song, drug, or experience to carry us through the day. Although music is calling us to respond, we ignore it and go on with something else in the hope that it would not wound our soul and expose us. We are vulnerable and fragile, looking for truth in a song that reflects our experience or what we think we want in life. Truth and love uncovers who we really are without hurting us. Love and truth in music is uplifting to the soul. It connects us emotionally to the singer and songwriter. Love in music is not self-seeking like Marvin Gaye's song, "Sexual Healing". Love in music does not delight in evil or self-centeredness, like many rap artists have portrayed in their songs. A true artist is one who sings songs that convey a message not of despair, hate, or prejudice, but communicates in a way that they connect with all people, not just those of a certain segment of society. There is a very fine line in defining what is good music and what is not. Good music for sure last decades, and people always come back to hear more of that song.

However, the current Y generation, those born in 1980s, are being exposed to music that lacks solid creativity and depth, especially rap music. Yet there are advocates who believe, for example, that rap is good music. Jeff Mendleman says the following:

"Here's my equation: Mainstream rap music (=) what sells in America (x) the urban youth experience. Why urban youth experience? Rap music is primarily an urban youth-created art (although suburban whites consume most of it). As one rapper put it, "If you never had money growing up, and then all of a sudden you are surrounded by wealth, what would you rap about?" The American urban youth experience, especially for people of color, is one of scarcity. But, America values wealth – we hold up people like Bill Gates and Mark Zuckerberg as paragons of the American dream – and so, money sells. And paradoxically then, even if you don't have money, you rap about it. Next, why does rap music have violence? Inner-city America is caught in a violent battle. Urban youth of color witness the worst of it. Murder is normalized in their lives, and so, it's normalized in their songs, too. Last, why does rap have misogyny? Men are in power in America. Couple that with the fact that in urban youth environments, positive male role models are hard to come by,

and a tragic, self-perpetuating cycle emerges. What youth observe in mainstream media, they perform in their real life, which cycles back into mainstream media. In fact, many rappers cite being "raised by the streets" or the television. So, rap music as a genre, doesn't necessarily promote bad values, but right now, it has a lot of them".[35]

When taken as a whole, the culture of pop music today is lacking in many ways. It does not have the creative writing team of those who came out of the 1950s and 1960s. Although there are many great singers today, the overall quality of sustaining professionalism is not there. Finally, as a passing note, one group of Generation X that came out of the Southwest produced a song that truly resonated with young people and especially college students. The vocal group, The Latinos, and their very much-loved song "When the Party's Over" combine classic strong harmony vocals with a spiritual message of hope.

---

[35] http://mic.com/articles/3001/from-jay-z-to-kanye-west-does-rap-music-promote-bad-values

PART FIVE

FINDING MY ECHO

16

ALBUMS, PHOTOS, PEOPLE, AND EVENTS

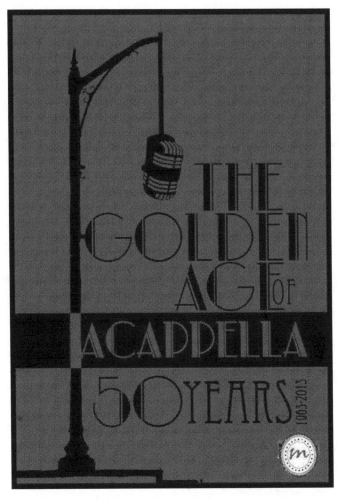

Commemorating 50 years of Acappella as a pop genre

Joe Calamito (Heartaches) and Herman Hamond (Royal Counts)

Stan and Ewa Krause -Courtesy Reena Rose Sibayan- The Jersey Journal

The Shantons featuring Skip Jackson

(Rich Zielinski archives)

Destinaries   Islanders

The Chessmen today (Courtesy Ziffer archives)

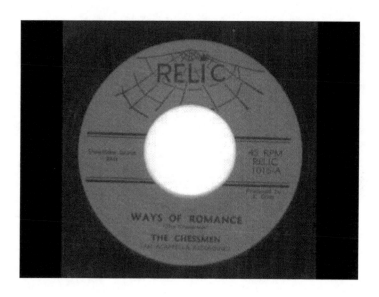

Stan Krause Record shop

Rich, Stan Tommy & Joe

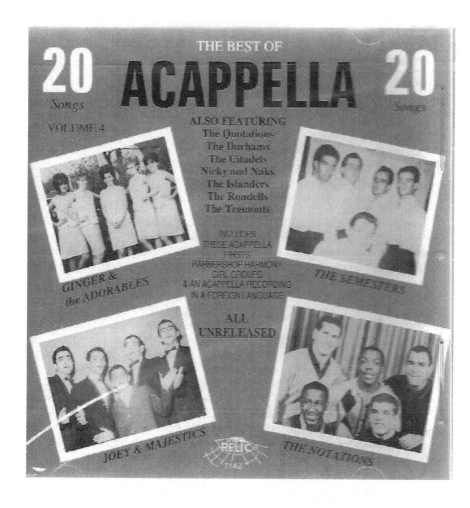

THE TIMETONES   TIMES SQUARE RECORDS

DANCING IN THE STREET
THERE HE IS (AT MY DOOR)

MARTHA and the VANDELLAS

GORDY-7033

DON K. REED

A longtime CBS/FM personality, Don K. Reed has collected a devoted following through his weeknight program on the Golden 101. However, it's Sunday night when Don K. pulls out all the stops.

For five hours on the "The Doo-Wopp Shop", Don K. gives exposure to a mixture of standard Doo-Wopps, some of the lesser-known old sides as well as contemporary Doo-Wopp recordings. "I really like 'The Doo-Wopp Shop'," he says. And it's evident that Don K.'s audience shares his enthusiasm as the program generates enormous listener involvement.

Don K. Reed's success in the New York Market as THE authority on the New York "Doo-Wopp" sound isn't surprising. A bona fide New Yorker, Don K. grew up in Brooklyn during the 1950's where and when group harmony was at its very peak.

Don K. blends his knowledge of the 50's artists and sounds with his familiarity of the New York audience. "The Doo-Wopp Shop" and the Don K. Reed Show are THE shows for New York's adults...and the advertisers who want those adults to listen and respond.

solid gold music
WCBS FM101

14 Karat Soul

***

Class of 57

Author and historian on rhythm and blues Marv Goldberg

(Goldberg archives)

Contenders

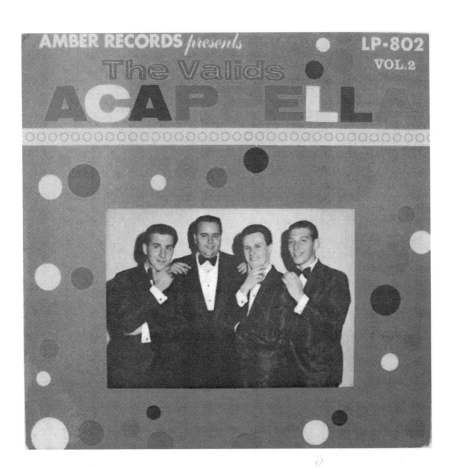

RKO Fordham Theater- Bronx, New York

(Courtesy of Lehman College Library)

2 Smooth

The Bonairs (George Scott Archives)

Sparrows

Gus Gossert New York City –DJ

State Theater home of acappella shows

(Jersey City Free Public Library-John Beekman MLIS)

Acappella shows at the Fox Theater Hackensack, New Jersey

(Circa early 1960s https://www.pinterest.com)

RON LUCIANO and STAN KRAUSE Present:

. . . A C A P P E L L A   S H O W . . .

The Zircons — The Savoys — Five Sharks

The Del-Capris—The Meadowbrooks—The Delicates

M. C. RON LUCIANO

Added Attraction — The What-Nots

FOX THEATER

309 Main Street, Hackensack, N. J.

TUESDAY NITE, NOVEMBER 9, 1965

Show Starts 8:30

ALL WELCOME!!   DONATION: $2.00

No 016   No 016

(Courtesy of www. Richard Nader.com)

17

TEENS, YOUNG ADULTS, AND SOULFUL ARTISTS

The Vribteors

(Courtesy of Stan Krause archives)

Dixie Cups

The Chessmen

THE SCHOOLBOYS

The School Boys

Autumns

The Heartaches

Prime

Golden Acappella Records
Presents Volume 1

"The 5 Jades"

"The Past is in the Future"

THINGS TO COME

VOCALS IN ACAPPELLA

GENE MINOR (718) 949-2357   AL CROWD (718) 465-2295

Twilights

Camelots

Image

The Valentines

The Echelons

2 Smooth

Neal Stuart of the Zirkons

The Lyrics

THE DELICATES

Skyhawks

Wayne Stierle

Carmen The Doo Wop Corner

Broadcasting from down under- South Australia on

93.7FM

Acappella

Well, the 60s are gone, and so is my "Chevy", my hair is grey and I'm pretty heavy. The 1960s are a thing of the past, street corner harmony was really a blast. My record collection is as large as can be, Persuasions, Five Fashions, Chessmen and Sharks, Zircons, Heartaches, Concepts and Larks. Between you and me and my 45, my record collection is still alive. I don't care what people say, acappella is here to stay.

SOULFUL ARTISTS

First Hispanic (Puerto Rican) on the Motown Label

Booker T. & The M.G.s successful integrated band

First non-black artist on the Motown label

Italian-American Soulful Singer

Soulful entertainer Angel Rissof

(Paul Undersinger Photography)

18

CHART AND TIMELINE

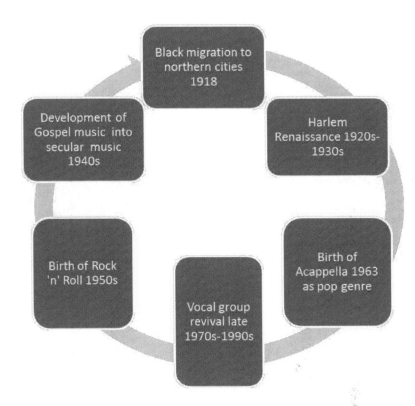

THE PROMOTION OF VOCAL GROUP HARMONIZATION INCLUDES SOME OF THE FOLLOWING:

TV Shows

Radio

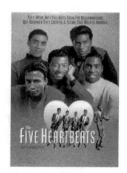
Film

Plays

19
CONTEMPORARY VOCAL GROUPS

Talk of the Town

Silk City

Quite Storm

(Photo courtesy of http://classicurbanharmony.net/)

Lola and the Saints

Pentatonix

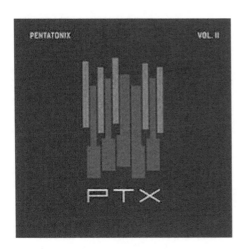

(Photo credit Bobby Holland)

Nota

First Acappella winners of NBC The Sing Off

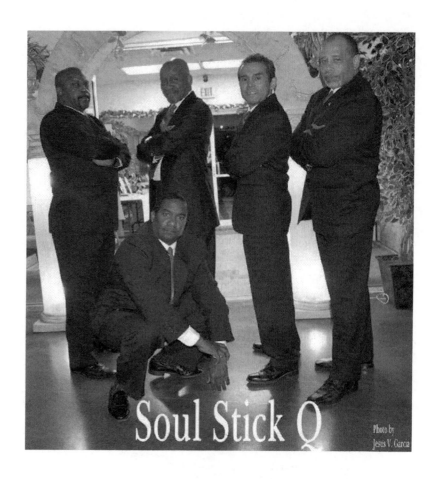

Soul Stick Q

Photo by
Jesus V. Garcia

IBU first Asian R&B group to win the New York's
International Music Festival in

2005

Choice- The Bad Boys of Jersey City

Larry Chance and The Earls

The Whiptones
Sh'Boom

The Whiptones
Doo Wop A Cappella Quartet

20
JERSEY CITY ON THE HUDSON

GOLDEN DOOR INTERNATIONAL FILM FESTIVAL
2011

Joe Calamito (The Heartaches) Ted Ziffer (The Chessmen)

Editorial Reviews

"BLACK GROOVES"
ARCHIVES OF AFRICAN AMERICAN MUSIC & CULTURE

Based on the commentary and personal memories of a wide array of accomplished acappella musicians, Street Corner Harmony tells the story of doo-wop on the street corners of Philadelphia, Jersey City, and New York City in the 1950s and '60s. The film features modern-day footage of the cities so loved by the former street musicians, allowing viewers to explore the back alleys of the East Coast that became "concert halls" for these burgeoning adolescent musicians. The endearing men who tell their stories are still passionately involved in the performance of acappella music—and they've still got it! The music is great and the stories recall the nostalgia of teenagers in the 1950s and their drive to make an impact on their neighborhoods.

The question of race was deliberately unimportant when these young men of all creeds and colors were seen on the same corner, enjoying a cathartic and rejuvenating afternoon of acappella performance. This color-blind fervor for acappella is what makes their story even more universally appealing and important, focusing on groups like The Persuasions, Five Jades, Chessmen, and many more. Former members of The Concepts (an early '60s acappella group that recorded on the same label as the more prominent Persuasions) and the producer, director, and writer of the film, Abraham J. Santiago, beautifully bridge the gap between doo-wop and rock 'n' roll in this valuable account of acappella street corner harmony.

Reviewed by Rachel Weidner

Nominee for Best Documentary

Beautiful Jersey City on the Hudson

Bob Waters (The Five Fashions) Abe Santiago

The Heartaches- Tommy D'Alessandro & Joe Calamito

Reno and Lisa Costa & Robert & Rose Garcia

Juan Perez original member of the Concepts

Steve Willette-The Five Chancells- Tony O Dungen, and Eddie Black-Five Sharks

(Photo TNT North Jersey Rhythm and Blues Party)

Jim Reeves- Master Recording Engineer

Friends and supporters who love classic R&B group sound

21

DISCOGRAPHY

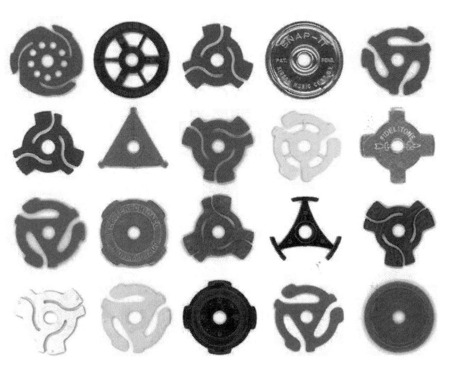

ACAPELLA Groups of the 1960s

Ad-Libs (Recorded the hit: "The Boy from New York City")
Apparitions

1. Atlantics

2. Attitudes

3. Avenues

4. Babraroso & the Historians (Aka: Nicky Addeo with Ray & The Darchaes) Barons (Aka: The Pretenders & Kook Tones)

5. Bon-Aires

6. Boutiques (Unrecorded female group)

7. Camelots (Recorded the hit "Pocahontas")

8. Candelites

9. Chantons

10. Chessmen

11. Chevieres

12. Chimetimes (Aka: Reunion)

13. Chris & The Cytations

14. Citadels (Featuring Dennis Ostrom, Later of the Vibraharps, & Blue Sky Boys)

15. Compulsions

16. Concepts

17. Contenders (Aka: Lytations, 5 Scripts, 5 Shits - Lead Jack Strong)

18. Cordials

19. Count Five

20. Creations

21. Crowns

22. Del Capris

23. Del Stars

24. Del Vons

25. Destinaires

26. Destinations

27. Distinctions

28. Durhams

29. Du-Vells

30. El-Sierros (Aka: Tearstains, Tommy & The Tears, Knick Knocks & Vi-Tones Emeralds (Unrecorded female group)

31. Excellons (Aka: The Excellents "Coney Island Baby" fame)

32. Five Chancels

33. Five Embers

34. Five Fashions (Aka: A Group Called Us)

35. Five Fortunes

36. Five Jades

37. Five Latins (Aka: The Concepts)

38. Five Scripts (Jack Strong-Lead, also The Lytations, 5 Shits, Contenders & Zeppers)

39. Five Shadows (Aka: The Five Jades)

40. Five Sharks

41. Formations

42. Fortells

43. Four Clefs (Aka: The Consorts on Cousins Label - Sal Donnarumma's group)

44. Four of us (Unrecorded group)

45. Gents

46. Ginger & The Adorables (Aka: The Lynettes)

47. Heartaches (Aka: Joann & The Heartaches)

48. Holidays

49. Horizons

50. Hudsons

51. Illusions

52. Islanders

53. Joel & The Autumns (Joel Katz - Lead)

54. Joel & The Conchords (Joel Katz - Lead)

55. Joel & The Rhondells (Joel Katz - Lead)

56. Kacties

57. Kathy & The Connotations

58. Knick Knacks

59. Knick Knocks (Aka: El-Sierros, Tearstains, Tommy & The Teats, Vi-Tones)

60. Kool Tones (Aka: The Pretenders & Barons)

61. Louaires

62. Lynettes (Aka Ginger & The Adorables)

63. Lytations

64. Majestics (Aka: Little Joe & The Majestics)

65. Meadowbrooks

66. Medallions (Unrecorded group) Memories

67. Metropolitans (Unrecorded group)

68. Monteys

69. Natural Facts

70. Nick & the Nacks

71. Noble Hearts

72. Notations (Aka: The Connotations on Technichord)

73. Nutmegs (Recorded the hit "Story Untold")

74. Progressions (Unrecorded group)

75. Potentials

76. Pretenders (Aka: The Root Tones & Barons)

77. Q-Tones

78. Quotations (recorded the hit "Imagination") Regencies

79. Relations (Aka: Kacties)

80. Reminiscents

81. Revlons

82. Rhondells

83. Rising Tide

84. Rituals

85. Royal Counts

86. Rue Teens

87. Sands

88. Satan & The Angels

89. Semesters

90. Shells (Recorded the hit: "Baby Oh Baby")

91. Sintells

92. Sparrows Quartet

93. Spirals

94. Splendids

95. Syndicates

96. Tearstains (Aka: El-Sierros, Tommy & The Tears, Vi-Tones)

97. Teen Five

98. Timetones (Recorded the hit "In My Heart") Tremonts

99. Uniques

100. Valids

101. Variations

102. Velvet Angels (Aka: Nolan Strong & The Diablos)

103. Versailles

104. Vibraharps (Aka: Vibraniques)

105. Vibraniques (Aka: Vibraharps)

106. Vibratones

107. Vic & The Gents (This group recorded the rarest acappella 45)

108. Youngones

109. Zeppers

110. Zircons (Manhattan group - The first Zircons group to record)

111. Zirkons (Bronx group)

1. AD-LIBS – New Jersey
LPs

1967   Acappella Records Inc. LP 1001

"New York to La Acappella All The Way"

1967   Human

1968   New York in the Dark

2. APPARITIONS – New York

1965   Relic LP 103 – "The Best of Acappella Vol. 3"

1969   Park of Our Love

1966   Relic LP 105 – "The Best of Acappella Vol. 5"

1966   Relic LP 108 – "The Best of Acappella Vol. 6"

Image of A Girl Since I Fell for You

1967   Relic LP 109 – "Best of Acappella Vol. 7"

1970   Forgotten Spring

1971   Don't Leave Me Baby

1972   Autumn Leaves

3. ATLANTICS – New Jersey
1967   Acappella Records Inc. LP 1001 "New York to LA, Acappella All The Way"

Every Boy and Girl

Now That The Thrill is Gone

Grand Hotel

Be Sure You Know

Beans

4. ATTITUDES – New York
45s

1966   Times Square 110

That Old Black Magic

Mama's Doin The Jerk

5. AVENUES – New Jersey
LPs

1967 Snowflakes L 1001 – "The Stars of Acappella Vol. 1"

Oh Ginny

6. BARAROSO & THE HOSTORIANS – New Jersey

1965   Jade 120

Zoom

When I Fall in Love

7. BARONS – New York

1965   Relic 101 "The Best of Acappella"

When You Dance

8. CAMELOTS – Brooklyn, NY

45s

1962   Aanko 1001

1962   Don't Leave Me Baby

1963   Don't Leave Me Baby

1964   Cameo 334

1965   Crimson 1001

Don't Leave Me Baby

The Letter

1966   Relic 530

Chain of Broken Hearts

1966   Relic 541

Dance Girl

LPs

1965   Relic 101 "The Best of Acappella"

9. CANDELITES – New Jersey

1967 Snowflake 1001 "The Starts of Acappella Vol. 1"
She Don't Wanna Love Me

10. CHANTONS – New Jersey

1967 Snowflake 1001 "The Starts of Acappella Vol. 1"

Where or When My Girl

I Wonder Why

Trickle

1967 Snowflake 1002 "The Starts of Acappella Vol. 1"

When You Wish Upon a Star

When You Dance

11. CHESSMEN – New York, NY

45s

1966 Relic 1015

I Apologize

Dance

1966 Relic 1016

Ways of Romance

Heavenly Father

1966 Relic 107

That's My Desire

Starts Fall

1966   Relic 1020

Love is What The World is Made of

Don't Have to Shop Around

LPs

1965   Relic 101 "Best of Acappella"

Heavenly Father

Two Kinds of People

For All We Know

1965   Relic 102 "Best of Acappella Vol. 2"

I Want to Dance

Let Me Come Back

A Teardrop

Is Everybody Happy

Sentimental Reasons

1966   Relic LP 105 "Best of Acappella Vol.5"

Ooh Baby Baby

Danny Boy

1966   Relic LP 106 "Acappella Showcase Presents The Chessmen"

There Goes My Baby

Ways of Romance

I've Been Good to You

All Night Long

Dance

Don't Have to Shop Around

That's My Desire

I Want to Dance

Flowers on The Wall (Splat) Pt. 1

You Know My Heart is Yours

Love is What The World is Made of

Stars Fall

For All We Know

Dance Gypsy

A Teardrop

When We Were So in Love

Is Everybody Happy

I Apologize

Flowers on The Wall (Splat) Pt. 2

The One Love Forgot

12. CHEVIERES – Pittsburgh, PA

LPs

1967   Relic LP 109 "The Best of Acappella Vol. 7"

Uncle Sam

Last Night I Dreamed

13. CHIMETIMES – New Jersey

LPs

1968   Snowflake LP 1004 "Acappella Battle of the Groups" What's Your Name?

14. CHRIS & THE CYTATIONS – New Jersey

45s

1963   Catamount 100

Unbelievable

Glory of Love

LPs

1965   Cat-Time 201 "I Dig Acappella"

Zing

15. CITADELS – New York

LPs

1965   Relic 102 "Best of Acappella Vol. 2"

New Love Tomorrow

When I Woke Up This Morning

When I Fall In Love

1965   Relic LP 103 "Best of Acappella Vol. 3"

Tonight I Fell In Love

Pennies From Heaven

Dream World

1966   Relic LP 104 "Best of Acappella Vol. 4" I'll Never
        Let You Go

1966   Relic LP 104 "Best of Acappella Vol. 5"

        Earth Angel

16. COMPULSIONS – Philadelphia, PA

1967   Pantomime 2003 "Philadelphia's Greatest
        Acappella"

        What's Your Name?

        The Fairest

17. CONCEPTS – Jersey City, NJ

45s

1966   Catamount 112

        Yo Me Pregunto

        The Vow

        Crystal Ball 1110

        When We Get Married (Live) released 2010

LPs

1966   Cat-Time 202 "I Dig Acappella Vol. 2"

        Our Anniversary

18. CONTENDERS – Philadelphia, PA

45s

1967   Whitney Sound 1929

Gunga Din

Wake Up in the Morning

19. CORDIALS – New Rochelle, NY

LPs

1968   Catamount CLP 902

My Love For You

I'm on The Outside Looking In

Island of Love

Steal Away

Duke of Earl

Love No One But You

Everybody Says

Young and in Love

I Do

If I Should Lose You

I Laughed

Teardrops

So Much in Love

Traveling Stranger

Over The Rainbow

20. COUNT FIVE – West Orange, NJ

(Aka: The New Count Five)

    45s

    1966   Nason 101 (4-song EP)

          Please Say It Isn't So

          At The Candy Store

          It was Acappella Music

          Standing on The Corner

    LPs

    1966   Relic 103 "Best of Acappella Vol. 3"

          I Do Believe

          Bells of Love

          There Was a Time

    1966   Relic LP 105 "Best of Acappella Vol. 5"

          Sound of Heartbreak

Recording as: THE NEW COUNT FIVE

    1967   Snowflake 1001 "The Stars of Acappella Vol. 1"

          I Want Some One

          No Time for You

          So Much in Love

          Temptation Walk

    1967   Snowflake 1002 "The Stars of Acappella Vol. 2"

          May I

I Want a Girl

It's Growing

1968   Snowflake 1004 "Acappella Battle of the Groups"

She Blew a Good Thing

Juke Box Box-set Early 70''s – Standing on The Corner

21. CREATIONS – Pittsburgh, PA

LPs

1967   Relic LP 109 "Best of Acappella Vol. 7"

Through Eternity

My Best Friends Girl

22. CROWNS – New Jersey

LPs

1967   Snowflake 1001 "The Stars of Acappella Vol. 1"

Your Way

Little Star

I Know

1967   Snowflake 1002 "The Stars of Acappella Vol. 2"
I Need You

23. DEL CAPRIS - Jersey City, NJ

45s

1966   Amber 854

Up On The Roof

If I Should Lose You

1966   Catamount 115

Teardrops Follow Me

Man in the Moon

LPs

1965   Acappella Unlimited 791 Vol. 1

Sincerely

Cruise to the Moon

My Hero

Up On The Roof

Sunny Side of the Street

One More Time

Til There Was You

Traveling Stranger

Stormy Weather

Sweeter Than

Two Kinds of People

For Sentimental Reasons

I Want Your Love

One Summer Night

1966   Amber LP 801

Gee Whiz

I Should Get My Head Examined

So Much in Love

24. DEL STARS – New York

45s

1964   Mellomood 1001

For Your Love

Zoop Bop

1964   Mellomood 1004

Why Do You Have To Go

Who Said You Wasn't Mine

LPs

1965   Relic 101

Zoop Bop

1965   Relic 102

Your Way

25. DELVONS – New York

45s

1967   J.D.F. 760

Stay Clear of Love

Please Stay

26. DESTINAIRES – Bronx, New York

45s

1965 Old-timer 602

Traveling Stranger

1965 Old-timer 609

Rag Doll

Teardrop

1965 Old-timer 610

Chapel Bells

It's Better This Way

1965 Old-timer 613

More

Diamonds & Pearls

1965 Old-timer 614

You're Cheating On Me

1966 Siamese 407

More

Diamonds & Pearls

27. DESTINATIONS – Philadelphia, PA

LPs

1967 Pantomime 2003 "Philadelphia's Greatest Acappella"

The Sun's Message

Funny Feeling

Hey Boy

28. DISTINCTIONS – Philadelphia, PA

LPs

1967   Pantomime 2003 "Philadelphia's Greatest
Acappella"

Token of Love

I Want to Dance

No Time for You

29. DURHAMS – Philadelphia, PA

45s

1966   Relic 1018

Seconds of Soul

Sincerely

LPs

1966   Relic LP 103 "Best of Acappella Vol. 3"

Maureen

This is My Love

Don't Say We're Through

30. DU-VELLS – New Jersey

LPs

1968　Snowflake 1004 "Acappella Battle of the Groups"

Bye Bye Baby

31. EL-SIERROS – New York

45s

1964　Time Square 29

Love You So

Valerie

1964　Times Square 101

Life is but a Dream

Pretty Little Girl

1966　Relic 527

Picture of Love

LPs

1965　Times Square 201 "Sounds of the City Album"

Sometime I Wonder Our Love is a Vow Glory of Love

This is Night

Over The Rainbow

Walking Alone

32. EMERALDS – Jersey City, N J

My Prayer (Unreleased)

33. EXCELLONS – Bronx, NY

45s

1964   Bobby 601

Sunday Kind of Love

Helene (Your Wish Came True)

1965   Old-time 601

Sunday Kind of Love

Helene (Your Wish Came True)

1965   Relic 101

Sunday Kind of Love

34. FIVE CHANCELS - Bronx, NY

45s

1965   Dawn 302

Love No One But You

Please Let Me Love You

1965   Fellatio 103

Love No One But You

1966   Rendezvous 1001 (EP)

Gee But I'm Lonesome

LPs

1966 Pantomime 2002 "Acappella Classics Vol. 2"

You're Driving Me Mad

Book of Love

All Night Long

1967 Snowflake 1002 "Stars of Acappella Vol. 2" Gee But I'm Lonesome

LPs

1966 Pantomime 2002 "Acappella Classics Vol. 2" You're Driving Me Mad

Book of Love

All Night Long

1967 Snowflake 1002 "Start of Acappella Vol. 2" Gee But I'm Lonesome

35. FIVE FASHIONS – Stamford, CT

(Aka: A Group Called Us)

45s

1965 Catamount 102

Pennies From Heaven

10 Commandments of Love

1965 Catamount 103

Solitaire

Over The Rainbow

1978 Catamount 116 (1960s recording... 65-66) After New Year's Eve

LPs

1965 Cat-Time 201 "I Dig Acappella"

Diamonds & Pearls

This I Swear

Comes Love

10 Commandments of Love

Stormy Weather

1966 Cat-Time 202 "I Dig Acappella"

Never Never

Something On Your Mind

36. FIVE FORTUNES – Philadelphia, PA

LPs

1967 Pantomime 2003 "Philadelphia's Greatest Acappella"

That's My Desire

Stay

37. FIVE JADES – Bronx, NY

45s

1965 Your Choice 907/908

My Reverie

Rosemarie

1965 Your Choice 909/910

My Girlfriend

How Much I Love You?

LPs

1966 Relic LP 108 "Best of Acappella Vol. 6"

Shout

Rosemarie

1966 Relic LP 107 Five Jades "Velvet Soul For Lover's Only"

How Much I Love You

If I Were to Lose You

If Someone Would Care

That's The Way It Goes

Are You Sorry

I Wish You Love

I Wish I Fall In Love

Unchained Melody

My Reverie

Begin the Beguine

Endless night

I Was Such A Fool

Ebb Tide

In The Still of the Night

Tell Her That I Love Her

That's My Desire

1967   Relic LP 109 "Best of Acappella Vol. 7"

My Girlfriend

When You Dance

38. THE FIVE SHADOWS – Bronx, NY

(Aka: The Five Jades)

45s

1965   Mellow mood 011/012

Don't Say Good Night

Sunday Kind of Love

1965   Relic 102 "Best of Acappella Vol. 2"

10 Commandments of Love

39. FIVE SCRIPTS – Philadelphia, PA

45s

1965   Script 57-5103

My Friends Tell Me

You Left My Heart 1968 Long fiber 201

The Clock

Peace of Mind

40. FIVE SHARKS – Bronx, NY

45s

1964   Old-timer 605

Stand By Me

I'll Never Let You Go

1965   Old-timer 611

Gloria

Flames

1966   Amber 852

The Lion Sleeps Tonight

Land of 1000 Dances

1966   Rendezvous 1001 EP

Good Lovin''

1966   Siamese 404

Gloria

Flames

1966   Siamese 405

Stand By Me

I'll Never Let You Go

1966   Siamese 410 EP

Possibility

Remember Me Baby

Lost Love

So Much In Love

1966 Crystal Ball 1110

Up on the Roof –released 2010

LPs

1965 Cat-time LP 201 "I Dig Acappella"

Little Girl (You're Gonna Belong to Me)

1966 Cat-time LP 202 "I Dig Acappella"

Young Boy Blues

Old Man River

You'll Never Walk Alone

Is Everybody Happy

1966 Amber 801 "The Stars of Acappella"

The Lion Sleeps Tonight

Land of 1000 Dances

1966 Pantomime 2002 "Acappella Classics Vol. 2"
Teardrops Follow Me

Blue Moon

Will You Love Me Tomorrow?

Somewhere

1967 Snowflake 1002 "Stars of Acappella Vol. 2"

Happy Teenager

41. FORMATIONS – New Jersey

LPs

1967   Snowflake 1001 "Stars of Acappella"

Mexico

My Juanita

1967   Snowflake 1002 "Stars of Acappella"

My Girlfriend

I Love You

1968   Snowflake 1004 "Acappella Battle of the Groups"

Oh Gee Oh Gosh

42. FORTELLS – New Jersey

45s

1965   Catamount 109

Exodus

Return to Me

LPs

1966   Cat-Time LP 202

Old Black Magic

I Believe

Danny Boy

43. FOUR CLEFS 45s

1966   BJ 1000

Please Be Mine

Time After Time

44. FOUR OF US – New Jersey

(Aka: Rising Tide)

1968   Unreleased

There's a Moon Out Tonight

Denise

This Is My Love

Bench in the Park

45. GENTS – New York, NY

45s

1963   Times Square 2

Island of Love

1963   Times Square 4

I'll Lever Let You Go

46. GINGER & THE ADORABLES – West Orange, NJ

1966   Relic LP 104 "Best of Acappella Vol. 4" He's Gone

47. HEARTACHES – Jersey City, NJ

45s

1966   Catamount 114

I'm So Young

A Lover's Call

LPs

1971   Catamount 906 "Lamppost Love Songs"

(1960s recordings: 66-68)

A Lover's Call

My Vow to You

So Much In Love

Pennies From Heaven

Valerie

Change of Heart

Gee Whiz

Uncle Same

I'm So Young

Tears on My Pillow

Tonight I Fell In Love

He's Gone

April

I'm So Young (With music)

48. HOLIDAYS 45s

1966   Relic 542

This I Swear

Summertime

LPs

1965   Relic 102 "Best of Acappella Vol. 2"

Chant of the Isles

Adios

My Baby Loves Me

It Happened Today

Time After Time

49. HORIZONS – New York

LPs

1965   Relic LP 103 "Best of Acappella Vol. 3"

Why Did You Make Me Cry

1966   Relic LP 104 "Best of Acappella Vol. 4"

A Story of Love

1968   Snowflake 1004 "Acappella Battle of the Groups"
Blue Moon

50. HUDSONS – West New York, NJ

1967 Acappella Records, Inc., LP 1001 "New York to
LA, Acappella All The Way"

Lucky Old Sun

Danny Boy

You're The Girl

Everybody's Got A Home But Me

Exodus

The Neighborhood

If I Love You

51. ILLUSIONS – Philadelphia, PA

1967 Pantomime 2003 "Philadelphia's Greatest Acappella" (You'll Lose) A Precious Love

Beauty's Only Skin Deep

52. ISLANDERS – Long Island, New York

LPs

1965 Relic LP 103 "Best of Acappella Vol. 3"

My True Story

Hey Hey Baby

1966 Relic LP 104 "Best of Acappella Vol. 4"

Walking in the Rain

1966 Relic LP 105 "Best of Acappella Vol. 5"

You Never Loved Me

1966 Relic LP 108 "Best of Acappella Vol. 6

When We Get Married

53. JOEL KATZ VOCAL GROUPS – New Jersey

54. JOEL & THE AUTUMNS

45s

1966 Amber 856

Never

Exodus

1967 Power N871

Never

Exodus

LPs

1966 Amber 801 "The Stars of Acappella"

Never

Exodus

1967 Snowflake 1002 "Stars of Acappella"

Lorraine

1968 Snowflake 1004 "Acappella Battle of the Groups"
Over The Rainbow

55. JOEL & THE CONCHORDS – New Jersey

45s

1966 Amber 850

Hurry Home

Moonlight in Vermont

LPs

1967   Snowflake 1004 "Stars of Acappella Vol. 2"
Lovers Quarrel

One Summer Night

1968   Snowflake 1004 "Acappella Battle of the Groups"
It Happened Today

56. JOEL & THE RHONDELLS – New Jersey

LPs

1968   Snowflake 1004 "Acappella Battle of the Groups"
Maureen

57. THE KACTIES – Brooklyn, NY

45s

1966   Kape 702

Donald Duck

Over The Rainbow

LPs

1966   Relic LP 108 "Best of Acappella Vol. 6"

What Did I Do Wrong?

Over The Rainbow

The Rest of My Life

58. KATHY & THE CONNOTATIONS – New York

LPs

1966   Pantomime 2002 "Acappella Classics Vol. 2"

      Uncle Sam

      Why Do Fools Fall In Love

      Once Upon a Time

      KNICK KNOCKS

1965   Times Square 201 "Sound of the City"

      Alka Seltzer

      Temptation

59. KOOLTONES 45s

1965   Relic 101 "Best of Acappella"

      Traveling Stranger

60. LOUAIRES – New York

LPs

1967   Snowflake 1001 "Stars of Acappella Vol. 1"
      Stormy Weather

1967   Snowflake 1001 "Stars of Acappella Vol. 2"
      Chant of the Isles

      I Do Believe

61. LYNETTES – New Jersey

LPs

1967   Snowflake 1001 "Stars of Acappella Vol. 1" When I'm With Him

1967   Snowflake 1002 "Stars of Acappella Vol. 2"

If You Were Gone From Me

1968   Snowflake 1004 "Battle of the Acappella Groups" He's So Fine

62. LYTATIONS – Philadelphia, PA

LPs

1966   Times Square 107

Over The Rainbow

Look Into the Sky

63. MAJESTICS (Little Joe & The) – New York, NY

LPs

1966   Relic LP 104 "Best of Acappella Vol. 4"

Every day of the Week (with Little Joe)

Ave Maria

I'm So Young (with Little Joe)

1966   Relic LP 105 "Best of Acappella Vol. 5"

Twilight (with Little Joe)

This Magic Moment (with Little Joe)

64. MEADOWBROOKS – New Jersey

45s

1965   Catamount 106

Time After Time

Seems Like Only Yesterday

1965   Catamount 108

Lovers Quarrel

Is Everybody Happy

LPs

1966   Cat-Time 202 "I Dig Acappella Vol. 2"

Ways of Romance

In The Still of the Night

Congratulations

65. MEDALLIONS Jersey City, N J

Follow Your Heart (Unreleased)

66. MEMORIES – New York

LPs

1965   Times Square 201 "Sound of the City"

Stop, Look, and Listen

67. METROPLOITANS (Unrecorded group)

68. MONTEYS – New York

1965   Time Square 201 "Sound of the City"

If You Love Me

Teardrops

69. NATURAL FACTS – Philadelphia, PA

LPs

1967   Pantomime 2003 "Philadelphia's Greatest Acappella"

The Clock

Lost Love

70. NICK & THE NACKS – New York

1965   Relic LP 103 "Best of Acappella Vol. 3"

A Lovely Way to Spend an Evening 1966 Relic LP 104 "Best of Acappella Vol. 4"

White Cliffs of Dover

1965   Relic LP 105 "Best of Acappella Vol. 5"

Good Good Bye

71. NOBLE HEARTS – New Jersey

1968   Snowflake 1004 "Acappella Battle of the Groups"
Beating of My Heart

72. NOTATIONS – New Jersey

45s

1966   Relic 10109

Danny Boy

You Can Run

Crystal Ball 1110

(Danny Boy Live) released 2010

LPs

1966   Relic LP 104 "Best of Acappella Vol. 4"

Lost Love

For Your Precious Love

Kentucky Blue

1966   Relic LP 105 "Best of Acappella Vol. 5"

When I Fell In Love

Hang On Sloopy

1966   Relic LP 108 "Best of Acappella Vol. 6"

My Foolish Heart

1967   Relic LP 109 "Best of Acappella Vol. 7"

Peace of Mind

73. NUTMEGS POTENTIALS – Philadelphia, PA

LPs

1967   Pantomime 2001 "Philadelphia's Greatest Acappella"

She Cried

The Letter

74. PRETENDERS – New York

1966   Relic 101 "Best of Acappella"

Pennies from Heaven

75. Q-TONES – Philadelphia, PA

1966   Pantomime 2003 "Philadelphia's Greatest Acappella"

Gloria

Crazy Bells

76. QUOTATIONS – Brooklyn, NY

45s

1970   Relic 1020 (60s Recordings)

Imagination

Ala Men Sy

LPs

1965   Relic LP 103 "Best of Acappella Vol. 3"

I Wonder Why

I've Seen Everything

Maybe You'll Be There

1966   Relic LP 104 "Best of Acappella Vol. 4" I'll Be
Home

Why Do You Do Me Like You Do

1966   Relic LP 105 "Best of Acappella Vol. 5" I Don't
Want To Cry

To The Aisle

1966   Relic LP 108 "Best of Acappella Vol 7"

Imagination

Ala Men Sy

77. REGENCIES – Philadelphia, PA

1967   Pantomime 2003 "Philadelphia's Greatest
Acappella"

Bewitched

Don't Stop

78. RELATIONS – Brooklyn, NY

(Aka: The Kacties)

45s

1966   Kape 703

What Did I Do Wrong?

Too Proud To Let You Know

79. REMINISCENTS – New Jersey

1967   Relic LP 109 "Best of Acappella Vol. 7"

Oh Let Me Dream

Hey You

80. REVLONS – New York

LPs

1965   Time Square 201 "Sound of the City"

I Lost My Job

81. RISING TIDE – New Jersey

1968   Snowflake 1004 "Acappella Battle of the Groups"
You'll Forget Me

California Dreaming

Closer Step by Step

The Lion Sleeps Tonight

82. RITUALS – New York

45s

1966   Rendezvous 1001 EP

Juke Box Saturday Night

LPs

1966   Cat-Time LP 2002 "I Dig Acappella Vol. 2"
Sea of Love

Sorry, I Ran All The Way Home

1966   Pantomime 2002 "Acappella Classics Vol. 2"
You Never Loved Me

Since I Don't Have You

Stranger in Paradise

83. RONDELLS – New Jersey

LPs

1966   Relic LP 104 "Best of Acappella Vol. 4"

My Prayer

84. ROYAL COUNTS – Jersey City, NJ

45s

1966   Catamount 1958

Way Over There

That's How I Feel

Crystal Ball 1110

Cindy (Live) released 2010 LPs

1967   Catamount LP 901 "Royal Counts Acappella Soul"

My Girl

Don't Have to Shop Around

Don't Look Back

He's The One that Love Forgot

Made Up My Mind

Gypsy Woman

There Goes a Fool

When We Get Married

Farewell My Love

When You Wish Upon a Start

It's Growing

Time

I'll Always Love You

Peace of Mind

Too Young

Valerie

1977   Catamount 904 (Acappella Soul Vol. 2 (recorded in the 60s)

Introductions Song

Hey There Lonely Boy

Tell Him

That's How I Feel

Over The Rainbow

He'll Be Back

Way You Do The Things You Do

Fading Away

For All We Know

Chim Chim

Gypsy Whoa

No Man is an Island

I Want a Girl

85. RUE TEENS SANDS – Philadelphia, PA

LPs

1967   Pantomime 2003 "Philadelphia's Greatest
Acappella"

Gee, But I'd Give the World

Crying

86. SATAN & THE ANGELS – Philadelphia, PA

LPs

1968   Pantomime 2004 "Blue Eyed Soul-Acappella"
Never Let You Go

A Quite Place

Babelu's Wedding Day

There Goes My Love

Time Makes You Change

Let The Bells Ring

Rama Lama Ding Dong

Trenton's Medallion

Remember Then

When We Got Married

The Storm is Over

Gee

Will You Hold My Hand

87. SAVOYS – Newark, New Jersey

45s

1964   Catamount 101

If You Were Gone From Me

On What a Dream

1964   Catamount 780

Gloria

The Closer You Are

1965   Catamount 104

Crazy

When I Fall in Love

1965   Catamount 105

Gloria

The Close You Are

88. SEMESTERS – New Jersey

1966   Relic LP 104 "Best of Acappella Vol. 4"

Laura My Darling

Summer Nights

89. SHADOWS- Bronx, New York

1966   Crystal Ball 1110

Chapel Dreams (live) released 2010

90. SHELLS – Brooklyn, NY

LPs

1967   Snowflake 1000 "The Shells Sing Acappella"
Misty

So Fine

I'm on the outside looking in

Happy Holiday

Baby Oh Baby

The Closer You Are

Be Sure My Love

The Way You Do The Things You Do

Life is but a Dream

Baby Walk On In

Fine Little Girl

91. SINTELLS – New York

1966   Relic LP 105 "Best of Acappella Vol. 5"

Lundee Dundee

Please Say It Isn't So

1966   Relic LP 108 "Best of Acappella Vol. 6"

My Imagination

92. SPARROWS QUARTETTE – Brooklyn, NY

45s

1965   Jet 3000

Deep In My Heart

Love My Baby

93. SPIRALS – New York

1966   Relic LP 108 "Best of Acappella Vol. 6"

Peace of Mind

Adios My Love

94. SPLENDIDS – Staten Island, NY

1966   Cat-Time 202 "I Dig Acappella Vol. 2" Don't Leave Me Baby

1967   Pantomime 2002 "Acappella Classics Vol. 2" Oh Baby Baby

1968   Snowflake 1004 "Acappella Battle of the Groups" Could This Be Magic+

95. SYNDICATES – New York

45s

1966 Mello 552

Do What You're Gonna Do

The Duke

96. TEARSTAINS – New York

LPs

1965 Time Square 201 "Sound of the City"

Too Young

97. TEEN FIVE – New York

45s

1963 Time Square 2

Darling I Love You

1963 Times Square 4

Till The End of Time

1964 Time Square 98

Till The End of Time

1965 Times Square 99

Darling I Love You

98. TIMESTONES – New York

45s

1964   Times Square 26

Sunday Kind of Love

Angels in the Sky

99. TOMMY AND THE TEARS

(Aka: The Vitones & The Tearstains)

1965   Times Square 201 "Sound of the City"

Vows of Love

Punishment

Let Him Know

100. TREMONTS – Newark, NJ

1964   Relic LP 104 "Best of Acappella Vol. 4"

Merry-Go-Round Love

I Hear the Wind

101. UNIQUES – Brooklyn, NY

1966   Relic LP 105 "Best of Acappella Vol. 5"

It Was the Night

Speedo

Senorita

1966   Relic LP 108 "Best of Acappella Vol. 6"

The New Beat

1967   Relic LP 109 "Best of Acappella Vol. 7"

Dance

102. VALIDS – New Jersey

45s

1966   Amber 853

Blue Moon

Hey Senorita

1966   Amber 855

Congratulations

Barbara Ann

LPs

1966   Amber 801 "The Stars of Acappella Vol. 1"
Congratulations

Walking My Baby Back Home

Barbara Ann

Unchained Melody

This is My Love

My Foolish Heart

Blue Moon

1966   Amber 802 "The Valids – Acappella"

Over the Rainbow

Wonderful

Mexico

Mr. Lonely

Zing

Glory of Love

Kiss Kiss Kiss

Congratulations

Bartender

My Girl

The Closer You Are

When I Fall in Love

Up On The Roof

Boogalu Baby

Gloria

Begin The Beguine

103. VARIATIONS – Jersey City, NJ

LPs

1967   Acappella Records LP 1001 "New York to LA, Acappella All The Way"

Because of You

104. VELVET ANGELS – Detroit, MI

(Aka: Nolan Strong & The Diablos)

1965   Co-Op M201

I'm In Love

Baby I Wanna Know

1965   Medieval 202

Baby I Wanna Know

Since You've Been Gone

LPs

1972   Relic 5004 "Acappella Showcase Velvet Angels"

(1960s recordings)

For Sentimental Reasons

Mary

I Want to Know, Baby

Let Me Come Back

Be Every Wonderful

Since You've Been Gone

When You're Smiling

I'm In Love

Jungle Fever

Mary

Old MacDonald

Johnny Johnny

It's Too Soon to Know

105. VERSAILLES – New York

45s

1965   Harlequin 401

Little Girl of Mine

Teenagers Dream

1965   Old-Timer 607

Lorraine

I'm in the Mood for Love

1966   Rendezvous 1001 EP

Soft and Sweet

LPs

1965   Cat-Time 201 "I Dig Acappella"

Church Bells May Ring

To The Aisle

1966   Cat-Time 202 "I Dig Acappella Vol. 2" I'm Not a Know It All

Cecelia

1967   Snowflake 1002 "Starts of Acappella Vol. 2" Soft and Sweet

106. VIBRAHARPS – New York

(Aka: The Vibraniques)

LPs

1966   Relic LP 108 "Best of Acappella Vol. 6"

I Hear Bells

A Friend

Secret Love

1967   Relic LP 109 "Best of Acappella Vol. 7"

Talking to My Hear

VIBRATONES – Philadelphia, PA

LPs

1967   Pantomime 2003 "Philadelphia's Greatest Acappella"

I Do Believe

You Cheated

107. VIC & THE GENTS – New York

45s

1964   Doranna 1169/1170

Lydia

Sign From Above

108. VI-TONES –New York

45s

1964   Times Square 105

The Storm

Fall in Love

LPs

1966   Times Square 201 "Sound of the City"

109. WAYNE KELLY & THE EL CAMINOS – New York

45s

1965   Fellatio 101

Black Magic

Darling Can't We Take a Walk

110. YOUNG ONES – New York

45s

1964   Times Square 28

Gloria

Two Kinds of People

1964   Times Square 104

I Only Want You

Over the Rainbow

1966   Relic 527

Sweeter Than

1966   Relic 540

Gloria

Two Kinds of People

LPs

1965   Relic 102 "Best of Acappella Vol. 2"

Maryann

Shining Star

To Make a Long Story Short

111. ZIRCONS – Manhattan, NY

45s

1963   Mellomood 1000

Lonely Way

Your Way (with music)

112. ZIRCONS – Bronx, NY

(Also spelled ZIRKONS) 45s

1964   Cool-sound 1030

(I Hear) Silver Bells

You Are My Sunshine

1964   Old-Time 602

(I Hear) Silver Bells

1964   Old-Timer 603

Stormy Weather

Sincerely

1965   Old-Timer

Remember Then

You Baby You

1966   Relic 1008

Lonely Way

1966   Rendezvous 1001 EP

Here In My Heart

My Own True Love

1966   Siamese 403

Stormy Weather

Sincerely

1966   Amber 851

The Lone Stranger

One Summer Night

LPs

1965   Relic 101 "Best of Acappella"

Lonely Way

Silver Bells

Stormy Weather

1965   Cat-Time 201 "I Dig Acappella"

Remember Then

Unchained Melody

Blue Moon

1966   Amber 801 "The Starts of Acappella Vol. 1"
One Summer Night

The Lone Stranger

1966   Pantomime 2002 "Acappella Classics Vol. 2"
Crazy for You

Come Dance With Me

Never

1967   Snowflake 1002 "Stars of Acappella Vol. 2"

Here in My Heart

1968   Snowflake 1003 "Acappella Sessions with the
Zircons"

Stormy Weather

My Own True Love

Never

Smile

Remember Then

Crazy For You

You Baby You

Glory of Love

Silver Bells

Sincerely

Come Dance With Me

Sunday Kind of Love

Lone Stranger

The Wind

You Are My Sunshine

Once in a While

Here in My Heart

One Summer Night

45s

1962   Aanko 1001 Camelots

Don't Leave Me Baby

1963   Catamount 100 Chris/Cytations

1963   Mellomood 1000 Zircons

1963   Standard 100 5 Satins

1963   Times Square 2 Gents

1963   Times Square 4 Gents

1963   Times Square 6 Crests

1963   Times Square 6 Nutmegs

1963   Times Square 11 Memories

1963   Times Square 14 Nutmegs

1963   Times Square 19 Nutmegs

1963   Times Square 22 5 Satins

1964   Bobby 601 Excellons

1964   Cameo 334 Camelots

1964   Catamount 101 Savoys

1964   Catamount 780 Savoys

1964   Cool Sound 1030 Zircons

1964   Doranna 1169/1170 Vic & The Gents

1964   Times Square 36 Youngones

El Sierros

Picture of Love

1964   Times Square 94 5 Satins

1964   Times Square 97 Crests

1964   Times Square 98 Gents

1964   Times Square 101 El Sierros

1964   Times Square 104 Youngones

1964   Times Square 105 Vi-Tones

1965   Catamount 102 Five Fashions

1965   Catamount 103 Five Fashions

1965   Catamount 104 Savoys

1965   Catamount 105 Savoys

1965   Catamount 106 Meadowbrooks

1965   Catamount 107 Five Fashions

1965   Catamount 108 Meadowbrooks

1965   Catamount 109 The Fortells

1965   Co-op M201 Velvet Angels

1965   Crimson 1001 Camelots

Don't Leave Me Baby

The Letter

1965   Dawn 301 Traditions

The Wind

1965   Fellatio 101 Wayne Kelly & The El Caminos

1965   Fellatio 103 Five Chancells

1965   Jade 120 Barbaroso & The Historians

1965   Jet 3000 Sparrows Quartette

1965   Medieval 201 Velvet Angels

I'm in Love

Let Me Come Back

1965   Medival 202 Velvet Angels

Baby I Wanna Know

Since You've Been Gone

1965   Mellomood 011/012 Five Shadows

Don't Say Good Night

Sunday Kind of Love

1965   Old-Timer 602 Zircons

Silver Bells

Gino & The Destinaires

Traveling Stranger

1965   Old-Timer 606 Zircons

Remember Then

You Baby You

1965   Old-Timer 607 Versailles-New York

1965   Old-Timer 609 Destinaires

1965   Dawn 302 Five Chancells

1965 Harlequin 401 Versailles

1965 Old-Timer 610 Destinaires

1965 Old-Timer 611 Five Sharks

1965 Old-Timer 612 Rue Teens

Happy Teenager

Come a Little Bit Closer

1965 Old-Timer 613 Destinaires

More

Diamond & Pearls

1965 Old-Timer 614 Destinaires

1965 Times Square 99 Gents

1965 Times Square 102 Flamingos

1965 Times Square 103   Nutmegs

1965 Your Choice 907/908 Five Jades

1965 Your Choice 909/910 Five Jades

1966 Amber 850 Joel & The Conchords

1966 Amber 851 Zircons

1966 Amber 52 Five Sharks

1966 Amber 853 Valids

1966 Amber 854 Del Capris

1966 Amber 855 Valids

1966 Amber 856 Autumns

1966 B-J 1000 Four Clefs

1966 Catamount 112 Concepts

1966 Catamount 113 Fortells

Somewhere

Somewhere, Somewhere

1966 Catamount 114 Joann & The Heartaches

I'm So Young

A Lover's Call

1966 Catamount 115 Del Capris

1966 Fellatio 102 Traditions

1966 Fellatio 104 Five Sharks

1966 Fordham 109 Heartbreakers

1966 Kape 702 Kacties

1966 Kape 703 Relations

1966 Lana 128 Nutmegs

1966 Mello 552 Syndicates

1966 Nason 101 Count Five

1966 Relic 527 Youngones

1966 Relic 528 Nutmegs

1966 Relic 530 Camelots

1966 Relic 531 Nutmegs

1966 Relic 533 Nutmegs

1966 Relic 534 El Sierros

1966 Relic 535 Nutmegs

1966   Relic 540 Youngones

1966   Relic 541 Camelots

1966   Relic 1006 Nutmegs

1966   Relic 1008 Zircons

1966   Relic 1015 Chessmen

1966   Relic 1017 Chessmen

1966   Relic 1018 Durhams

1966   Relic 1019 Notations

Danny Boy

1966   Relic 1020 Chessmen

1966   Rendezvous 1001 Versailles

Here in My Heart

My Own True Love

Five Chancells

Gee, But I'm Lonesome

1966   Siamese 403 Zircons

1966   Siamese 404 Five Sharks

1966   Siamese 405 Five Sharks

1966   Siamese 407 Destinaires

1966   Siamese 410 Five Sharks

1967   J.O.F. 760 Del Vons

1967   Longfiber 202 Zeppers

1967   Power N871 Autumns

1967   Whitney Sound 1929 Contenders

1968   Candlelite 434 Nutmegs

1968   Gem 247 Give Embers

All Alone

Love Tears

1968   Long fiber 201 Five Scripts The Clock

Peach of Mind

113. ALBUMS / LPs

1965   Acappella Unltd. 701 Del Capris - Acappella Unlimited Vol. 1

1965   Cat-Time 201 I Dig Acappella

1965   Relic 101 Best of Acappella

1965   Relic 102 Best of Acappella Vol. 2

1965   Relic 103 Best of Acappella Vol. 3

1965   Times Square 201 Sound of the City

1966   Amber 801 Stars of Acappella Vol. 1

1966   Amber 802 Valids – Acappella

1966   Cat-Time 202 I Dig Acappella Vol. 2

1966   Pantomime 2002 Acappella Classics Vol. 2

1966   Relic 104 Best of Acappella Vol. 4

1966   Relic 105 Best of Acappella Vol. 5

1966   Relic 106 Acappella Showcase Presents The Chessmen

1966   Relic 107 Five Jades - Velvet Soul for Lovers

1966   Relic 108 Best of Acappella Vol. 6

1967   Acappella Records 1001 New York to LA Acappella All The Way

1967   Catamount 901 Royal Counts Acappella Soul

1967   Pantomime 2003 Philadelphia's Greatest Acappella

1967   Relic 109 Best of Acappella Vol. 7

1967   Snowflake 1000 Shells – The Shells Sing Acappella

1967   Snowflake 1001 Stars of Acappella Vol. 1

1967   Snowflake 1002 Stars of Acappella Vol. 2

1968   Catamount 902 Cordials – Acappella Blue Eyed Soul

1968   Pantomime 2004 Satan & The Angels – Blue Eyed Soul

1968   Snowflake 1003 Acappella Sessions with the Zirkons

1968   Snowflake 1004 Acappella Battle of the Groups

114. ACAPPELLA ALBUMS RECORDED IN THE MID 1960s & RELEASED IN THE 1970s

Catamount 904 Royal Counts Acappella Soul Vol. 2

Catamount 905 Persuasions Stardust

Catamount 906   Heartaches Lamp Post Love Song

Relic 5004 Velvet Angels Acappella Showcase Presents The Velvet Angels

115. ACAPPELLA RECORD LABELS 1960s-1970s

- Anako
- Acappella Records Inc.
- Amber
- B-J
- Bobby
- Cameo
- Candlelite
- Catamount
- Cat-Time
- Clifton
- Coo-op
- Cool-Sound
- Crimson
- Dawn
- Doranna
- Dream
- Fellatio
- Fordham
- Gem
- Harlequin
- Jade

- Jet
- J.O. F.
- Kape
- Lana
- Long fiber
- Medieval
- Mello
- Mellomood
- Nason
- Old-Timer
- Pantomime
- Power
- Relic
- Rendezvous
- Script
- Siamese
- Snowflake
- Whitney Sound
- Your Choice

116. POPULAR RECORD LABELS THAT PRODUCED VOCAL GROUPS IN THE 1980s AND BEYOND
(Not acappella exclusively)

- U.G.H.A.
- Starlight
- Avenue D
- Blue Sky
- Crystal Ball
- Monogram
- King Tut
- Popular Request
- Relic
- Robin Hood
- Pyramid
- Roadhouse
- Owl
- Arcade
- Greco
- Bab

22

ETHNOGRAPHIC DISCOGRAPHY

The discography here focuses on ethnic groups that were a part of rhythm and blues, soul, pop, folk, jazz and rock 'n' roll. Some of the recordings were done by vocal groups, individual singers, song writers and bands. Various ethnic groups played a part in advancing music as a whole. I have focused on three ethnic groups. Some were done with music and some were done without. This ethnographic discography is not complete, it is only a partial listing of songs done by various artist along the acappella corridor and beyond its borders.

Keep in mind that members of a vocal group or band does not make it an ethnic vocal group per se. Many singing groups were composed of diverse nationalities. This is the first taxonomy on vocal groups, singers, song writers and producers.

HISPANIC

- 1958 TNT# 153 Sonny Ace and the Twisters

- If My Teardrops Could Talk/ Swinging Stroll

- 1965 Dottie # 1130 Amber-tones

- I Need Someone/ If I Do

- 1965 Reprise # 0340 Blendells

- Dance With Me/ Get Your Baby

- 1963 Scarlet # 501 Blue Satins

- You Don't Know Me/ My Wife Can't Cook

- 1960 Harlem #111 Charlie and the Jives

- Mercy Baby/ Come On

- 1966 Catamount #112 The Concepts

- Yo Me Preguento /The Vow

- 1962 Renco # 3002 Dell Kings

- Big Mistake/ Just Remember

- 1961 Jox # 031 Dino and the Dell-Tones

- Don't leave me baby/ I'm Gonna Run

JEWISH

- 1970 Relic # 1020 Quotations

- Imagination/ Ala Sy

- 1961 Miracle # 849 Valadiers

- Greetings This is Uncle Sam/ Take a Chance 1964 Old timer # 605 Five Sharks

- Stand by Me/ I'll Never Let You Go

- 1958 ABC Paramount # 9921 Carole King

- Right Girl/Goin' Wild

- 1950 Chess # 1002 Doc Pomus 78"

- No Home Blues/ Send For The Doctor

- 1953 Peacock #1612 Leiber & Stoller

- Hound Dog/ Night Mare

- 1958 Dore # 503 The Teddy Bears-Phil Spector

- To Know Him Is to Love Him /Don't You Worry My Little Pet 1957 Decca # 9-30520 Neil Sedaka

- Laura Lee/ Showtime

- 1962 Columbia # 4-42656 Bob Dylan

- Mixed Up Confusion/ Corina, Corina

- 1962 AM Records # 1005 Herb Albert

- The Lonely Bull/ Acapulco 1922

- 1973 Atlantic # 10284 Bette Midler

- Do You Want To Dance? / Daytime Hustler

- 1964 Red Bird # 10-014 The Shangri-las

- Leader Of The Pack/ What Is Love

ITALIAN

- 1964 Jolly Hi Fi Records # J20268 Le Amiche

- Se Mi Vuoi Un Po' Di Bene (Chapel of Love)/ Un Giorno O L'Altro 1962 Rayna Records #509 Vito & the Salutations

- Gloria / Let's Untwist the Twist 1957 Joyce Records # 103 Crests My Juanita / Sweetest One

- 1962 Coed Records # Co 571 The Duprees My Own True Love / Ginny

- 1960 Spector Records #1210 Joey Dee & The Starliters Face of an Angel/ Shimmy Baby

- 1958 APT Records # 45-25005 The Elegants Little Star/ Getting Dizzy

- 1964 Catamount Records # 101 The Savoy's

- If You Were Gone From Me / Oh What A Dream

- 1966 Catamount Records #C114 Joanne & The Heartaches

- A Lovers Call / I'm So Young

- 1966 Amber Records # 854 The Del Capris

- If I Should Lose You / Up On The Roof 1960 Cameo Records # 175 Bobby Rydell Ding-A-Ling / Swingin' School

- 1962 Colpix Records # CP 630 James Darren Conscience / Dream Big

- 1970 Bizarre Records # 0967 Frank Zappa

- Tell Me You Love Me/ Would You Go All The Way For The U.S.A.?

Work Cited

Abraham, Santiago and Steven Dunham. Acappella Street Corner Vocal Groups A Brief History and Discography of 1960s Singing Groups. Glencoe: Mellow Sound Press. (2006).

Altschuler, G. All Shook Up. New York: Oxford. (2003).

Anthony, De Curtis and Holly George Warren. The Rolling Stone Illustrated History of Rock & Roll. New York: Straight Arrow. (1992).

Anthony, Gribin and Matthew, Schiff. Doo Wop- The Forgotten Third of Rock 'n' Roll. Iola: Krause Publishers. (1992).

Anthony, Gribin and Matthew, Schiff. The Complete Book of Do-Wop. Iola: Krause Publishers. (2000).

Awkward, M. Soul Covers. Durham: Duke University Press. (2007).

Bane, M. White Boy Singin' the Blues. Dallas: Penguin Books. (1982).

Baptistas, T. Echo of Rhythm and Blues Era. New Bedford: TRB Enterprizes. (2000).

Bell, C. East Harlem Remembered: Oral Histories of Community and Diversity. Jefferson: McFarland & Company. (2013).

Betrock, A. Girl Groups. New York: A Delilah Book. (1982).

Bradley, D. Understanding Rock 'n' Roll. Bristol: Open University Press. (1992).

Bruce, T. The Death of Right and Wrong. Roseville: Prima Publishing. (2003).

Burns, G. Jazz a History of America's Music. New York: Afred A. Knopf. (2000).

Cahill, T. The Gift of the Jews. New York City: Nan A. Talese. (1998).

Cahn, J. (2011). The Harbinger. Lake Mary: Charisma Media/Charisma House Book.

Dávila, A. Barrio Dreams: Puerto Ricans, Latinos, and the Neoliberal City: Berkeley: University of California Press (2004).

Deke, Sharon, Ben Spalding and Brody McDonald. A cappella. Alfred Music. (2015).

Dubois, N. The History of Times Square Records. New York: Lulu. (2007)

Duchan, J. Powerful Voices The Musical and Social World of Collegiate A Cappella. University of Michigan Press. (2012).

Emerson, K. Always Magic In The Air. New York: Penguin. (2005).

Evans, M. Ray Charles The Birth Of Soul. London: Omnibus Press. (2005).

Floyd, A. The Power of Black Music: Interpreting Its History from Africa to the United States. New York: Oxford University Press. (1995).

Friedwald, W. Jazz Singing: America's Great Voices From Bessie Smith To Bebop

And Beyond. New York: Da Capo Press. (1990).

Goff, J. Close Harmony: A History of Southern Gospel. University of North Carolina Press. (2002).

Goosman, S. Group Harmony: The Black Urban Roots of Rhythm and Blues. Philadelphia: University of Pennsylvania Press. (2005).

Goria, P. They All Sang on a Street Corner. Port Jefferson: Phillie Dee Enterprises, Inc. (1983).

Haralambos, M. Soul Music. New York: Da Capo Press. (1974).

Hoffmann, F. Encyclopedia of Recorded Sound. New York: Routledge. (2005).

Kelly, S. Behind The Curtains: Friesen Press. Victoria, BC (2011).

Keys, J. Du Wop. Chicago: Vesti Press. (1991).

King, J. What Jazz Is: New York: Walker Publishing Company. (1997).

Leight, A. The Vibe H istory of Hip Hop. New York: Three Rivers Press. (1999).

Lepri, P. The New Haven Sound. New Haven: United Printing. (1977).

Leslie, Alexander and Walter Rucker Jr. Encyclopedia of African American History. Santa Barbara: ABC CLIO. (2010).

Leszczak, B. Who Did It First? Great Rhythm and Blues Cover Songs and Their Original Artists. Scarecrow Press. (2013).

Martin, G. Making Music. William Marrow and Company, Inc. (1983).

Mellonee V. Burnim and Portia K. Maultsby. African American Music: An Introduction. 2nd ed. New York: Routledge. (2015).

Molina, R. Chicano Soul. La Puente: Mictlan. (2007).

Neal, M. What the Music said: Black Popular Music and Black Popular Culture. New York: Routledge. (1999).

Nisenson, E. Blue The Murder Of Jazz. Da Capo Press. (1997).

Pitilli, L. Doo Wop Acappella: A Story of Street Corner, Echoes, and Three Part Harmonies. Rowman & Littlefield Group (2016).

Propes, S. Golden Oldies A Guide to 60's Record Collecting. Radnor: Chilton Book Company. (1974).

Pruter, R. Doowop. The Chicago Scene. Urbana and Chicago: University of Illinois Press. (1996).

Rojek, C. Pop Music Pop Culture. Cambridge: Polity Press. (2011).

Rosalsky, M. Encyclopedia of Rhythm & Blues and Doo-Wop Vocal Groups. Lanham: Scarecrow Press. (2002).

Rudinow, J. Soul Music. Ann Arbor: The University of Michigan Press. (2013).

Santiago, A. The Untold Story United Group Harmony Association. Glencoe: Mellow Sound Press. (2014).

Schwartz, D. Start and Run Your Own Record. Label: Billboard Books. (1998).

Serrano, B. Puerto Rican Pioneers in Jazz, 1900-1939: Bomba Beats to Latin Jazz. Bloomington: iUniverse. (2015).

Southern, E. The Music of Black Americans –A History. New York: W.W. Norton & Company, Inc. (1997).

Szatmary, D. Rockin' In Time. Upper Saddle River: Prentice Hall. (1996).

Talalay, K. Composition in Black and White: The Life of Philippa Schuyler. New York: Oxford University press. (1995).

Tate, G. Everything But the Burden-What White People Are Taking From Black Culture. Broadway Books. (2003).

Toynbee, J. Making Popular Music. London: Arnold Publishers. (2000).

Tracy, S. Hot Music Ragmentation, and the Bluing of American Literature. Tuscaloosa: University of Alabama Press. (2015).

Vantoura, S. The Music of the Bible Revealed: Bibal Press. (1991).

Warner, J. Just Walkin' In The Rain: The True Story of Johnny Bragg & The Prisonaires. Renaissance Books. (2001).

Warner, J. American Singing Groups. New York: Billboard Books. (1992).

Whiteis, D. Southern Soul-Blues. Urbana: University of Illinois Press. (2013).

ABOUT THE AUTHOR

Abraham Santiago is a music historian and a vocal group enthusiast for over fifty years. He was once a former disc jockey in California on station KCSS 91.9 FM during the early to mid-70s. He is also a film producer and songwriter. His music has appeared on PBS in 2001 in the Emmy Award winning documentary film "American High", by producer J.R. Cutler. Santiago was a vocal group member of The Concepts during the 1960s acappella era. He is the recipient of The Best Book Award by Soul Patrol.com in 2006 with co-author Steven J. Dunham. In 2011, his film "Street Corner Harmony" was a nominee for Best Documentary Film at The Golden Door International Film Festival in Jersey City, New Jersey. Contact him at: msproductions66@yahoo.com

APPENDIX

HARMONY WITH GOD

Today we live in a troubled world. We can honestly say, that we are on a collision course worldwide. Our economy is in shambles our sense of security has been torn apart and our leaders seem to have no direction in leading our country. It appears that we are like sheep going to the slaughter. An insurmountable amount of lives has been lost by natural disasters, crime, disease, terrorism and no one is asking the real questions about life. Could there be a spiritual component to this worldwide chaos? Most people believe that life to some degree has a spiritual connection. Gospel music in which R&B emerged has always had a spiritual connection. The Afro-American experience is rooted in the hallowed union to the God of Abraham. This spiritual link displayed itself in many vocal styles, and it has always been associated with the God of heaven. It is in this context, that the God of the Holy Bible reveals himself through natural disasters, government upheavals and personal experiences. The experience of many people who have gone through trials and hardships has led them to repent and to trust in the living God of Israel. By genuine repentance and faith alone in Messiah Jesus, mankind can reconnect with the living God and have peace and harmony.

PEACE AND LIFE

God loves you and wants you to experience his PEACE. Since it was God's plan for us to experience peace, purpose and direction in our lives, why is it that most people have not experienced it?

"For I know the plans I have for you," declares the LORD, "plans to prosper you and not to harm you, plans to give you hope and a future. Then you will call upon me and come and pray to me, and I will listen to you. You will seek me and find me when you seek me with all your heart."

Jeremiah 29:10-13

SEPARATION FROM GOD

God created us to have a relationship with Him and to experience all that he has for us. He loves us just the way we are and accepts us for who we are. Yet, we have a choice to accept Him or reject Him. Unfortunately, our desire is to please ourselves. This choice created a separation from God.

"I have no peace, no quietness; I have no rest, but only turmoil."

Job 3:26

GOD'S REMEDY

God has provided the remedy. Therefore, we must make a choice.

"Come now, let us reason together, says the LORD. Though your sins are like scarlet, they shall be as white as snow; though they are red as crimson, they shall be like wool."

Isaiah 1:18

RECEIVE THE MESSIAH JESUS OF NAZARETH

Man is sinful and separated from a HOLY GOD. Sin results in a lack of purpose, direction, and peace. Only through Jesus can we receive forgiveness of SINS.

"Jesus answered, "I am the way and the truth and the life. No one comes to the Father except through me."

John 14:6

Repentance and faith alone in Jesus is the only way we can be in HARMONY WITH GOD. It is not through being good, giving to charity or attending religious services.

"The fool says in his heart, there is no God. They are corrupt, their deeds are vile; there is no one who does good. The LORD looks down from heaven on the sons of men to see if there are any who understand, any who seek God. All have turned aside, they have together become corrupt; there is no one who does good, not even one."

Psalm 14:1-3

"Or do you show contempt for the riches of his kindness, tolerance and patience, not realizing that God's kindness leads you toward repentance? But because of your stubbornness and your unrepentant heart, you are storing up wrath against yourself for the day of God's wrath, when his righteous judgment will be revealed. God will give to each person according to what he has done."

Romans 2:4-6

What is keeping you from experiencing his forgiveness and being in harmony with God?

INDEX

A

Abe Santiago	188, 286
Acappella Groups	292
Acappella Redefined	22, 89
Acappella Growth	44
Acappella Girl Groups	109
Ad-Libs	297
Adamson and McHugh	38
Aficionados	26, 61, 73
Afro-Filipino	55
Alan Freed	64
Albums	223
All-Black Group	189
All-Girl Group	189
All-White Group	120, 189
Ambassadors to Acappella	41
Anathema	52
Antidote	217
Apollo Theatre	64, 94, 141
Aretha Franklin	144, 150
Atlantics	292, 298
Attitudes	292, 298
Avenues	292, 298

B

Babelu's Wedding Day	337
Babraroso & the Historians	292
Baby Pack On	161
Bach	217
Baritone	89, 92, 93, 108, 180, 181, 184, 188, 190
Barrier of Race	78, 123, 145, 141, 152
Battle of the Groups	132, 189
Beatrice Johnson	112
Billy Bauer	157
Birth of Acappella	88
Blaxploitation Films	51
Blues	119, 129, 137

Boca Raton	171, 172, 174
Bon-Aires	292
Boroughs	91, 171, 176
Bowers Avenue	205
Boyz II Men	43, 181
Broadway	26, 93

C

Cadillacs	34, 121
Camelots	252, 292
Candlelite Label	34
Carole King	141
Casa	23, 43, 45
Cecilio Rodriguez	121
Chantons	292, 300
Chart	267
Chessmen	93, 123, 228, 246, 261
Chevieres	292, 302
Chicano Vocal Group	121, 122, 124
Children's Album	181, 185
Choral	89
Claudine Clark	108
Clay Cole	160, 173, 174
Coney Island Baby	293
Contemporary Vocal Groups	269
Contralto-Soprano	187

D

Danny Boy	301, 320, 324, 331
Darlene Love	150, 153, 165
Debunking the Professional Myth	73
Decca	31, 38, 365
Deke Sharon	43, 45, 46
Destinaires	293, 310
Devoshun	162
Dion & the Belmonts	132, 134
Discography	291
Donn Fileti	130
Donnarumma's Group	294
Durhams	293, 311

E

Eastern Seaboard   14, 116, 133
Edwin F. Rivera   187
Emeralds   22, 110, 114, 293, 313
Ethnic Groups   23, 31, 59, 94, 116, 120,
                                                123, 132, 205, 208, 210
Ethnic-Racial   23, 60, 64, 138
Ethnographic Discography   363
Events   223
Exodus   320, 324, 325

F

Father of Contemporary Acappella   45, 46
Female Blues Guitarist   54
Female Vocal Groups   94, 107, 108, 110, 112
Fileti   28, 59, 99, 130
Finding My Echo   222
First Acappella Recording   24
First Caucasian Vocal Group (Motown Label)   61
First Female Group to Record Acappella   110
First Hispanic (Motown Label)   262
First Non-Black (Motown Label)   264
First Acappella Winners (NBC)   275
Five Jades   123, 125
Flamingos   150, 157, 176, 187, 199
Frankie Lymon   75, 120

G

Gangs   205, 207, 208, 209
Gentrification of Rhythm and Blues   56
Geriatric Singers   102
Ginger & the Adorable Citadels   109, 110, 294, 295
Girl Groups during the Acappella Years   107
Godfather of Acappella   46, 54, 104, 179

H

Harborside   189, 190
Healing Power of Good Music   214
Hebrews   216
Herman Lubinsky   139, 140

Hispanic Contribution to Rhythm and Blues 119
History of Black Music 65
History of American Music 84, 90
Holland 51, 86, 274
Home of Acappella Shows 242
Hudson Sound 84
Husha Bye Again 171

I

Iberian Peninsula 120
Illusions 294, 324
Importance of Preservation and Development 63, 92
Independent Acappella Records 34, 40, 41, 74, 90, 95
Infection of Acappella 25
Instrumentation 27, 89, 214
International Film Festival 282
Introduction of Acappella 41, 90
Irving Slim Rose 28, 37, 38, 89, 130
Italian Connection to Rhythm and Blues 129

J

James Brown 51, 53, 95
Jerry Lawson 24, 46, 49, 77, 104, 179
Jersey City on the Hudson 82
Jesus 52, 53, 195, 196, 209
Jewish Impact on Rhythm and Blues 137
Jimi Hendrix 95
Jimmie Rodgers 57
Jive Five 94, 173, 199

K

Karat Soul 43, 44, 181, 234
Kings of Acappella 181

L

Larkings 60
Lawson-Arranged Tunes 180
Lindy Hoppers 20
Line Dancing 148

Lion Sleeps Tonight   318, 319, 334
Little Girl of Mine   364
Lola and the Saints   272
Lone Stranger   350, 351
Lorraine   364
Lost Love   318, 330, 331
Louaires   82, 295, 327
Love No One but You   305

M
My Angel of Love   122
Make Love, Not War   215
Madison   33, 40, 185
Mainstream   33, 38, 40, 137, 220, 221
Majestic   123,295,328
Male-Dominated   94, 107
Males   95,111
Marv Goldberg   74, 235
Mecca   162, 176
Mike Miller   156
Mulatto Music   56
Murray the K   64, 94, 175
Muscle Shoals   51, 88, 91, 95, 141

N
National Anthem   166
Nazis   16
Neal Stuart   256
Newark and Bowers Avenue   205
No Ordinary Love Affair   172
Nick and The Nacks   36, 295, 330
Norah Jones   55

O
Oldies   38, 62, 104, 105, 159
Onomatopoeic   138
Orchestra   28, 89, 90, 159, 161
Overlapping of Black Performers 59

P

Pentatonix	273
People	223
Phil Spector	150
Photos	223
Peter Wein	173
Picture of Love	312, 353
Pioneer of Acappella	44, 54, 60
Plays	268
Please Say It Isn't So	306
Please Stay	309
Please Let Me Love You	313
Please Say It Isn't So	340
Power of Good Music	214
Pretenders	295, 332
Prime	249
Professional Myth	73

R

Race	16, 31, 76, 78, 137
Race Music	140, 141
Racial Groups	31, 76, 78, 137
Racial-Ethnic	60, 119, 216
Raul Vicente	185, 186
Regional Sound	31, 34, 39, 42, 51, 54, 86, 95
Reintroduction of Acappella	41, 42
Resurgence of Acappella and Vocal Groups	39
Rhythm and Blues	119, 129, 137
Rising Tide	295, 321, 334
Rockapella	43, 44, 181
Roots of Acappella	12
Royal Counts	79, 93, 97, 110

S

Saint James	159
Save the Last Dance for Me	151
So in Love	217
Sexual Healing	214
Silk City	270

Skyhawks   259
Skyliners'   168
Smokey Robinson   58, 61
Soprano   108, 168
Soulful Artists   244
Sparrows   241, 296
Stan Krause   26, 30, 44, 79, 110, 130,
                                  184
Standard for Acappella   41
Sweet Honey in the Rock   116

T

Talk of the Town   43, 121, 179, 180, 269
Teenage Vocal Groups   73
Teens   244
The Beatles   42, 182
The Dells   77, 78
The Girl I Love   161
The Persuasions   25
The Valentines   253
The Vribteors   244
Timeline   267
Tina Turner   150
Tom Giacalone   159, 160
Twilights   251

J

Jerry Wexler   59, 141
Joe Neary   159, 171, 176

U

UGHA   164,185
Unrest   23
Upheaval   24, 60, 62

V

Various Ethnic   209, 210
Val Shively   194
Vietnam   24, 39, 51, 102, 161, 209

View Point of Acappella   90

W
Walking In the Rain   161, 324
Wall of Sound   150
WASP   16
Wayne Stierle   28, 34, 50, 104, 110, 130,
                                        131, 260

WBLS   157
WBNX 1380   29
WCAM   29
WCBS AND WPIX   40
WHOM   29
WINS   157
WKTU   162
WWCO   165
WWRL RADIO   174

Z
Zircons   184, 261, 297, 349, 351

Made in the USA
Charleston, SC
24 September 2016